Contents

Acknowledgements

Sometimes during the day I stop what I am doing and ask: why is that only the Western order, the European way of doing things, is legitimate? At these moments I have found my students at Goldsmiths' College most understanding. I am greatly indebted to many authors whose work I use, quote or discuss and who are fully acknowledged in the Notes. I am particularly grateful to the following friends for intellectual stimulus and emotional support while I have been writing this book: Ariella Altzman, Slavka Bartlitz, Philip Cohen, Eileen Jebb, Paul Maltby, Desa Phillipi, Tasneem Raja. I have received encouragement from Charles Batteson, Teresa Bergen, Martin Carey, Mark Hobart, Lucy Daw Lane, Robert Moore and others. Clive Harris, Michael Keith and John Solomos provided a forum for discussion and debate. I would also like to thank many other people whom I have known only briefly, (or not known at all). A few minutes with them has been enough to experience a rapport, based on a mutual recognition and a shared understanding of the loneliness of exile, the brevity and frailty of human existence, the warmth of comradeship and the necessity of struggle.

Acknowledgement (p.80)
'Heritage of England'
Michael Rosen

Education and the Ideologies of Racism

Madan Sarup

By the same author:
Marxism and Education, Routledge & Kegan Paul, 1978
Education, State and Crisis, Routledge & Kegan Paul, 1982
Marxism, Structuralism, Education, Falmer Press, 1983
The Politics of Multiracial Education, Routledge & Kegan Paul, 1986
An Introductory Guide to Post-Structuralism and Postmodernism,
Harvester-Wheatsheaf, 1988.

First published in 1991 by Trentham Books

Trentham Books
13/14 Trent Trading Park
Botteslow Street
Stoke-on-Trent
England ST1 3LY

British Library Cataloguing in Publication Data
Sarup, Madan
  Education and the ideologies of racism.
  1. Great Britain. Schools. Racism
  I. Title
  370.19342

  ISBN: 0 94 8080 46 9

Cover illustration by John Boak

Designed and typeset by Trentham Print Design Ltd, Chester
and printed in Great Britain by BPCC Wheatons Ltd, Exeter.

Introduction

This short book is an introduction to education and the ideologies of racism within it. Most books on education have been written on an interpersonal level, they focus on the classroom and usually offer practical advice to the teacher on topics such as teacher-pupil interaction, issues of language and curriculum development. I want to criticise those approaches that define racism as an individual, psychological problem that can be remedied by the promotion of cultural pluralism. In contrast with the dominant emphasis on the personal, the experiential and the individualist aspects, I want to stress the institutional, structural and political elements.

This text contains chapters on the links between education and social class; the problematic relationship between class, gender and race — and how this affects black pupils in schools; a discussion of the many racist ideologies that are being used against black people, and the analysis of one such ideology: multicultural education. I also look at one representative school subject in particular — art — so that I can discuss concretely some of the problems of the (multicultural and/or antiracist) curriculum.

There are also chapters which discuss the ideologies of imperialism and the 'nation', and how there has been a shift in thinking about 'race' in education. The links between education, ideology, and politics are then explored, and finally, in the last chapter, some policy recommendations are made for the reconstruction of education.

But where shall I begin? There is no such thing as a merely given, or simply available, starting point: beginnings have to be made for each project in such a way as to enable what follows from them...

After the Second World War, just before the migration of black people to Britain, the main educational debate in this country was about social class. Sociologists and others were concerned about the fact that working class children were failing in the education system. Implicitly they were asking the questions: why are there so many inequalities in society? This, then, was the debate that was taking place when the migrants came in the 1950s and 1960s. Let us begin, therefore, by focusing on class before we broaden out to consider the dynamics of 'race' and gender.

Chapter 1

Education and Class

I like stories. I spend a lot of time collecting them, reading them, and sometimes I make them up too.[1] I'm going to begin by telling you four well-known, 'traditional' stories. They are really attempts to explain working-class failure in the British education system.

The first story: the power of language

Basil Bernstein argues that there are two language systems which are on a continuum: there is the restricted code at one end and the elaborated code at the other.[2] The restricted code is particularistic, it is context bound (or 'indexical'). It depends a lot upon shared and taken-for-granted assumptions. In the restricted code meaning is implicit. The elaborated code is universalistic, it is context free. In other words, it does not depend upon shared or taken-for-granted assumptions. The elaborated code is (or is supposed to be) generally available and therefore explicit.

Bernstein links this theory of language with a theory of the family. He distinguishes between positional families and person-orientated families. In positional families decisions about interaction are made by reference to the formal position. (Why must you do that? Because I told you so! I'm your father!). In person-orientated families decisions depend on individuals' unique attributes. There is much more an emphasis on explanation. Now, there is a relationship between the restricted code and positional families, and the elaborated code with person-orientated families. Working-class families tend (as a consequence of the social relations of their cultural position), to develop a positional role system and the children are likely to use a restricted code. I should add that both types of families are, of course, determined by class. A code, an underlying generative principle is, in brief, a relationship between class, language and family.

1

Bernstein believes that schools are based upon an elaborated code and so working-class children who have learned the elaborated code experience feelings of cultural discontinuity between life at home and life at school. Thus most middle-class children can always be expected to perform more successfully in the present school system because the code around which the system is organized is that which is typical of middle-class family life.

Bernstein's work has quite rightly received a great deal of criticism.[3] One of the sad, unintended consequences of his work is that working-class language is often equated with inferior language. I think that we should realize that Bernstein's 'codes' are, perhaps, just different language styles and that the schools' emphasis on the elaborated code is a social convention. And if this is the case we can raise the question: instead of trying to change the children should we not change the schools?

The second story: the function of schooling.

Marxist sociologists of education are interested in the question: what functions does schooling perform for capitalism? They suggest that we should consider such things as educational provision, social relations in schools, the organisations of knowledge and the curriculum, the link between schooling and industry.

Samuel Bowles and Herbert Gintis argue that there is a structural 'fit' between the educational system and the economic order.[4] To put it briefly, schooling prepares individuals for (the world of) work. It forms the skills and attitudes that workers are supposed to have. Schools, they say, foster and reward certain personality traits: passivity, submission to authority, perseverence. These personality traits rewarded in schools seem to be rather similar to those connected with good job performance in the capitalist economy. On the whole creativity and imagination are not valued. Bowles and Gintis suggest that individual responsibility is emphasized for middle-class children and close supervision for working-class children. If you think about it most school work is very much like factory work: timed, fragmented, differentiated, meaningless, not in the control of the worker.

Pupils are socialized into relationships of dominance and subordination. Schools emphasize hierarchies. They socialize pupils into accepting hierarchies as normal; pupils and teachers are continually reminded about their place in the hierarchical structure. We all know, for example, the difference between a public school and a state school, a grammar school and a comprehensive, a university and a 'poly'. Bowles and Gintis believe that the current relationship between education and economy is ensured through not the content of education but its form. Education prepares students to be workers through a correspondence between the social relations of production and the social relations of education. In short, schooling is not for human liberation; schooling is to preserve and legitimate class based inequality.

Against Bowles and Gintis' theory of social reproduction through schooling it could be argued that schools are not mirrors that directly reflect the needs of capital. At the time Bowles and Gintis wrote their book they did not fully realize that capitalist social relations are inherently contradictory. Schools sort, select and legitimate, but sometimes the needs of capital may contradict the processes of legitimation. Their thesis about social reproduction is pessimistic; as resistance is a missing category in their book little is said about the possibilities of transformation.

The third story: the irony of self-damnation

Paul Willis argues that the struggle over authority in schools is really a fight between cultures. The state school is a central case of class conflict — and of social reproduction. On the one side there is the school, and on the other the counter culture. The working class 'lads' want money, clothes and excitement. They are aggressive, sexist and racist. They only come to school for a 'laff'. They are hostile to the 'ear 'oles' who listen to the teachers and get on with their academic work. The 'lads', however, associate mental work with being effeminate. What they admire is manual work because, in their view, that's what a real man does. The 'lads' desperately want to escape to the adult world of work. Of course, they don't choose a career, they drift from one unpleasant, arduous job to another. Sometimes they lighten the monotony by 'messing about' in the workshop — rather like the way they used to behave at school. The lads soon become disillusioned but by the time they realise that they are in a trap, it is too late. They have damned themselves.

Willis's book *Learning to Labour* movingly demonstrates how subordinate roles come to be taken on freely.[5] Coercion is unnecessary. The book illustrates the ways in which many pupils from working-class homes reject schools and all that they stand for. He suggests that some of the real functions of institutions work counter to their stated aims. Thus working-class pupils' dissociation from school actually achieves for the system its main objective — the placing of the lads 'voluntarily' in unskilled manual work.

> In the sense, therefore, that I argue that it is their own culture which most effectively prepares some working-class lads for the manual giving of their labour power we may say that there is an element of self-damnation in the taking on of subordinate roles in Western capi-

talism. However, this damnation is experienced, paradoxically, as true learning, affirmation, appropriation, and as a form of resistance.[6]

On the other hand, Willis argues that within the working class there is a creative self-making process which he calls cultural production, and that we need to understand the contradictions and resistances which prevent capitalism from working neatly. This emphasis is a corrective to the deterministic correspondence thesis of Bowles and Gintis, and the structuralist marxism of Louis Althusser.

Willis is right to distance himself from a vulgar determinism, but he leaps from the position that humans act thinkingly and creatively on their circumstances to the romantic view which sees any act of protest as constituting a resistance to capitalism. Consider a typical example of this (so-called) oppositional behaviour, 'messing about' and 'having a laff'. Joey, one of 'the lads', is talking about his father:

> He (his father) makes it all sound like a big fucking school, he makes it sound like this place ... We was talking about messing about, and the old lady says 'Well, you shouldn't mess about', and the old man says, 'We do!' ... he told us about this bloke, got this other Paki, and fucking pulled his trousers down and pulled him round the shop by his cock, like, got him by the cock and fucking yanked him round the shop, all silly things like that. You could pull him and he might fall into the furnace or fall under a fucking hammer. He says you go under and you put a, not the spade end the other end of the shovel, and you put that under their legs and pick 'em up, pick 'em up fucking under there like [indicating crotch] ... and they can't get off. He reckons they're always fucking about like this, like and I thought it must be just like an extension of school, fucking working in factories, with the same people, the same people every day ...[7]

Here a father is justifying racist bullying to his son and the laff is against Asian workers. This must suit management; it is preferable that workers take time off from production to torment other workers than to call a mass meeting. One can hardly call this sort of thing 'resistance'.

The fourth story: the destruction of dignity

Another explanation for working class failure in the education system has been related by David Hargreaves in his book *The Challenge for the Comprehensive School* [8]. Unlike other sociologists who have blamed the child, the home or the family's social background, Hargreaves focuses on the school.

He begins his argument by a consideration of the erosion of working- class culture. There was a time when most working-class people lived in an extended family, worked in the local area and enjoyed a sense of community. There was social integration and, then in the 1950s, vast changes began to occur... The extended family changed its form. The economy (based on the local dockyard, the coalmine, the steel factory) has collapsed. There is chronic unemployment especially amongst the young. Those workers that are in work are being deskilled. Instead of the street community there is the anonymity of the New Town, or the loneliness in the high rise flat. In short, there is no clear, stable working-class world. Identity, too, is fragmented. It is in such a context that the new youth subcultures emerged: the Mods and Rockers, Skinheads and Punks. These working-class youth cultures provide opportunities of exploring different options, they are symbolic attempts to resolve social contradictions.

But why do working-class kids create their own solidarity groups against teachers? Hargreaves' argument is that the 'hidden curriculum' destroys the dignity of pupils. Young people react by producing a counter culture, which is an attempt to gain dignity. What has happened is that the comprehensive school is still dominated by the old grammar school curriculum. There are many types of skill, Hargreaves argues, aesthetic-artistic, affective-emotional, personal-social, physical-manual, but because of the dominance of grammar school norms only the cognitive-intellectual is valued. There has been a rapid growth in public examinations. Amongst other things this means that everyday life and experience of the pupils is excluded from the classroom, and only that knowledge which is assessible is stressed. In other words, the curriculum of the minority has become the diet of the majority. It is not surprising then that the majority of the working class experience failure. Hargreaves then suggests that instead of asking 'what kind of individuals do we want? we should ask: what sort of society do we want?

The meanings of social class

In the above section I have taken for granted the importance of social class but I haven't explained what it is. Class has different meanings for different groups of people. Marxist views of class are very different from those used by traditional sociologists and market researchers.

The empirical view of class is held by many 'professional' sociologists and others; they usually use a scale (developed by the Registrar General) where *occupations* are classified into major categories: social class I and II include professional and managerial occupations; social class III contains non-manual and skilled manual; semi-skilled occupations are in class IV; and unskilled in social class V.

There are many problems with this view of class. There are questions about categorization and definition: what jobs are skilled? semi-skilled? unskilled? This is a difficult question because as deskilling takes place, the concept 'skill' is continually changing.[9] According to this scale people's social class categories change as their jobs alter. Moreover, many parents in social classes IV and V may have their 'mobile' daughters and sons counted in different groups.

In this view social class is about the descriptive grouping of people. Class is conceptualized as a tool to measure something — it's all to do with numbers and percentages. Many sociologists have devoted their entire lives to refining and working within this empirical approach.

Karl Marx's conception of class has nothing to do with statistics, it is to do with relations of domination and subordination. In *The Paris Manuscripts, The Poverty of Philosophy* and *The Communist Manifesto*, Marx saw the proletariat and the bourgeoisie as the main classes of modern society[10]. In these early writings Marx saw the proletariat and the bourgeoisie as the two decisive classes of modern society, and the proletariat as the universal negation of alienation. This model derives its force not from the analysis of 'surplus value' embedded at the heart of his mature theory, but from a philosophical understanding of social development. Even in this simple two-class model it is clear that class for Marx was not defined in terms of occupation, income or consumption but related to the mode of production.

According to Marx a mode of production consists of the forces of production and the relations of production. The *forces* of production refer to the means of production and labour power. The *relations* of production refer to the relationship, for example, between the slave and the master, the serf and the lord, the proletariat and the bourgeoisie.

It is the mode of production that constitutes classes. In the capitalist mode of production there is a separation of the producer from the means of production and a concentration of the means of production, indeed a monopoly, in the hands of the bourgeoisie. This means that there is a class which has no means of subsistence other than the sale of its labour power — the proletariat. Class, then, is an *economic* relation between those who own the means of production and those who have to sell their labour power and are exploited.

Class, to put it briefly, is a relationship of exploitation. By exploitation I mean the appropriation of part of the labour of others; in a commodity-producing society this is appropriation of what Marx called 'surplus value'. It should be noted that the individuals constituting a given class may or may not be wholly or partly conscious of their own identity and common interests as a class.

In a mode of production there are contradictions between the forces of production and the relations of production. Now, there can be economic crises within modes of production, but this does not necessarily imply a confrontation between classes. The two may or may not fuse. The mode of production and class struggle are always at work but we should remember that the second must be activated by the first.[11]

We can say that class *conflict* is essentially the fundamental relationship between classes, involving *exploitation* and resistance to it, but not *necessarily* having class consciousness or collective activity in common, political or otherwise, although these features are likely to supervene when a class has reached a certain stage of development and become what Marx once called 'a class for itself'.[12]

In short, Marx's mature theory is not mono-dimensional; class is never a single, homogenous structure, but rather a cluster of groups which, sharing similar work, functions, values, aspirations, interests, will frequently diverge on particular specific issues. It follows that class consciousness is dialectical in its development and contradictory in structure. Working-class consciousness is not a given datum but is created in struggle and struggle can take many forms.

Some sociological aproaches

There is no doubt that working-class childen do less well in education than middle-class children but why is this and how does it happen? Many studies have shown clear class differences in educational achievement. Let me give you a few examples. Children's reading scores were found to vary according to the social class of their parents. At age seven the proportion of children showing reading problems in social class V was more than five times that of class I.[13] In maths it was found that higher levels of skills were associated with more affluent areas. Needless to say it is the same story when one considers performance in public examinations. Very few university entrants are from semi-skilled and unskilled occupation categories. Halsey's studies showed that the chances of a working-class pupil going to a university in the 1960s were virtually no better than those of his parents 30 years earlier.[14] There are, then, clear class differences at every stage of education.[15]

Some researchers explain this by saying that working-class people are culturally and linguistically deprived. Others contend that working-class culture is different — but that doesn't necessarily mean that its inferior. Many argue that blame should not be put on pupils and their families; it may well be that the current *school system* itself contributes towards class differences (Hargreaves). And some writers believe that though factors inside the school are important, political and economic factors outside the school are the most significant (Bowles and Gintis). How, then, is working-class underachievement to be explained? Are working-class pupils genetically inferior or are they, or their parents, or both, just not motivated towards educational 'success'? Do schools alienate working-class pupils? Or is it something to do with low teacher expectations and the labelling of working-class children? Perhaps the state, and its educational institutions, actually discriminates against working- class people?

Some of the interactionist and marxist approaches that are sometimes used to answer such complex questions can usefully be outlined here. I will state the main features of these approaches, indicate their strengths and weaknesses and then assess their contribution to our understanding of schooling.

The interactionist approach

Symbolic interactionism was a reaction against the dominant structural-functionalism of the 1950s. The latter approach (sometimes called the 'normative paradigm') is associated with the work of Talcott Parsons, Robert Merton and other Americans. It assumed a value system that was agreed by everyone. It emphasised society rather than the individual, social stability rather than social change. Human beings were heavily socialised into the system. According to structural functionalism, sociology was seen as neutral or value free; education simply had 'functions'.

Symbolic interactionism, on the other hand, stressed not society but the individual. It emphasised consciousness and intention, the purpose of agents, their meaningful activity. Individuals were not just passively socialised, they negotiated, bargained and were capable at times of individual resistance. Radicals espoused symbolic interaction because it focused on the poor and the powerless. Interactionism has a great humanistic appeal. Sociologists like Harold Becker want to help the underprivileged. They are also against prediction and control: i.e. scientism.

In the sociology of education, interactionism transferred attention from the education system to the school, particularly to interaction within the classroom. There was a tendency towards description, ethnography, rather than forms of explanation. I think that 'labelling' theory was an advance in teachers' understanding.

The main criticisms of this approach are that it focuses only on the interaction of individuals and small groups. It looks at schools and classrooms in isolation from society — if you look at the early work of David Hargreaves or Colin Lacey you will see what I mean — but we know that the determinants of inequality lie outside the education system. Symbolic interactionism has no concept of class and ideology, it has no theory of the state and of its apparatuses.

The expansion of interactionism led to an interest in phenomenological sociology. Though there is continuity between these approaches there is an important difference: whilst symbolic interactionists believe that there is a real world, phenomenological sociologists hold that mind not matter is primary. The mind creates and changes reality. In phenomenology, then, the emphasis is on consciousness, choice, interpretation. (Some sociologists of education went further and took up ethnomethodology, an approach which focused on language and rules of making sense).

The main strength of phenomenology is, of course, its challenge to positivism. In the sociology of education the phenomenological approach is exemplified in the work of Michael F.D. Young and his associates.[16] This approach focused on the curriculum. It asked the question: why do some school subjects have high status and others have low status? They argued that knowledge and how it is transmitted are political questions. The curriculum reflects the distribution of power. They were against hierarchies and wanted to shift the emphasis from the teacher to the pupil, from the written to the oral, and from the theoretical to the practical.

What were the positive features of this approach? Firstly, it supported progressivism, secondly, it made concepts like 'knowledge', 'ability', etcetera problematic; and thirdly it argued that 'cultural deprivation' was a myth. But in spite of its many positive features phenomenological sociology of education did run into many problems. I think this was largely because these theorists held that one could change oppressive arrangements by a change in consciousness. In other words, this approach stressed a cultural radicalism which was divorced from political and economic understanding. Phenomenology stresses the consciousness and the subjectivity of the agent, the experience of the actor. It is voluntarist and idealist. Ultimately, the phenomenological approach leads to relativism.[17] Concepts like class are seen as reifications and so there is no understanding of the class struggle. Phenomenological sociology has no theory of power; it has no understanding of the forces of production and the social relations of production — the economic base.[18]

The humanist approach

Faced with the problems that I have outlined above many radicals began to study marxism seriously. The sort of marxism studied tended to be the humanistic marxism that one associates with the young Lukács. Lukács was a phenomenologist before he was a marxist and this meant that he saw Marx phenomenologically. Lukács drew heavily on Hegel and his idea that mind has superiority. Everything is an expression of the epoch, and society is seen as having an 'essence'. In Hegelian marxism there is a notion of base and superstructure; everything manifested in society is an expression of an inner essence. (What the essence is varies according to the theorist.) For Lukács the 'essence' was the class consciousness of the proletariat. He always stressed the voluntarist element, the notion that the class makes itself. When one thinks of humanist marxism in contemporary Britain one thinks of the work of Edward Thompson and Raymond Williams. Another example — in the field of education — is the work of Paulo Freire.

As this approach stresses the importance of 'lived' experience and human agency, teachers feel they can do something but the main problem with this approach is that the conception of society, the social formation, tends to be simplistic and 'essentialist'. Indeed, most humanist marxists tend to have a *deep suspicion* of the economic base.

The economist approach

Another marxist approach, with a different view of the base/superstructure, is associated with Friedrich Engels and the Second International. In this view of the social formation the 'base' is conceptualised as being strong and powerful and the superstructure as a mere epiphenomenon. The dynamic between base and superstructure is undirectional and the processes seen as laws. This approach is sometimes rigid and crude because the mediations are missing; there is no notion of contradiction in the Diamat.[19]

I think that this is the underlying view of the social formation assumed by Samuel Bowles and Herbert Gintis in their book *Schooling in Capitalist America*. To the older generation of sociologists of education what Bowles and Gintis are saying must be quite shocking: the education system is not the means by which social inequalities can be overcome but is the means by which it is perpetuated. 'Education' may be an unproblematic good, but what youngsters are undergoing is *schooling*. Schools form different personality types which correspond to the requirements of the economic system. Schools reproduce the labour force and legitimate inequality. Schools are alienating, they do not foster personal development but actually limit it. Bowles and Gintis believe that what teachers teach is not very important, it is the *form* that matters; the hidden curriculum is political. In short, there is a correspondence between the social relations of schooling and those of production.

Criticisms of Bowles and Gintis' 'correspondence' theory are well known. Their thesis is so deterministic that teachers are helpless. They feel that there is nothing that they can do. The determinism arises from their view of the base/superstructure relationship. The mechanistic reductionism of Bowles and Gintis prevents them from realising that the education system is heterogeneous and contradictory. The locus of control in education is nowhere specified. Moreover they have a pluralist theory of the state. It could be said that their view is influenced by structural-functionalism; perhaps that is why they have no notion of contradiction between school and production, between base and superstructure.

The structuralist approach

Structuralist marxism, exemplified in the work of Louis Althusser, challenged both the humanist view associated with Lukács and the mechanistic economistic one that is said to derive from Engels. In this approach the social formation is theorised as a structure of levels, the economic, the political, the ideological and theoretical. These levels of 'practices' are separate but interrelated, and there are contradictions within and between the levels which can be in different phases from each other. The base determines and is determined; the relationship between the base and superstructure is that of relative autonomy. The social formation (society) is not just a matter of intersubjective relations between people; we are bearers, 'supports' of the mode of production. Althusser goes on to argue that empiricism neglects the contradictions that exist below the surface. The deeper levels cannot be experienced, they can only be grasped by the construction of concepts.

He makes an important distinction between the repressive state apparatus and the ideological state apparatuses and insists that ideology is material, that it is embedded in institutions and institutional practices and has real effects. In the field of education the Althusserian approach has emphasised that 'education' is now the dominant ideological state apparatus. It teaches people 'know-how', some technical and social skills; education also defuses, depoliticises, and perpetuates dominance. 'Education' in this view became a sort of 'soft-policing'.

Numerous criticisms have been made of Althusser from many different directions. It has been said that this approach is formalist, functionalist and theoreticist. It polarises, on the one hand, a mass of subjects-in-ideology and, on the other, the bearers of science, the vanguard intellectuals of the party.

The 'ethnographic' approach

Bowles and Gintis and Althusser are 'social reproduction' theorists. Their views on the functions of schooling are similar. Both approaches tend to be deterministic because they do not have any conception of resistance. Practising teachers in urban schools know that students do not accept their compulsory schooling passively. Many working-class youngsters resist the norms of the school. Paul Willis has written in *Learning to Labour* how 'the lads' reject school knowledge, but in rejecting intellectual work they, ironically, reproduce the mental/manual division in society.

Why is Willis' work so popular and influential? I think there are several reasons. Some of his theories have been taken up by many sociologists of education because they needed a counter- balancing argument to break out of the pessimistic determinism of the Bowles and Gintis thesis and the structuralist marxism of Althusser. I think Willis tends to romanticise the working class; every activity of 'the lads', messing about, 'having a laff' is seen as if it were oppositional to capitalism. Though he emphasises working-class resistance the tragic irony is that the bloody-mindedness of 'the lads' leads to their own entrapment. Willis' story is in the end as deterministic as that of Bowles and Gintis. One thing we can learn from this debate is to use the word 'resistance' much more carefully. Perhaps we should make a distinction between resistance that is individualistic, 'residual' and that resistance which is collective, 'emergent', organised and progressive?

Another criticism of Willis' work is that there is no reference to the school being determined by internal struggles, or reflecting wider political struggles. The school is presented as if it were separate from the class system. In my view the power of an institution like the school is a product of class relations. A capitalist institution does not represent merely the interest of the institutional regime or the ruling class but it is also *the expression of the relationship between the classes.*

Willis' work is also important in that his notion of 'resistance' has been used by sociologists as a supplement to Braverman's account in *Labour and Monopoly Capitalism* to theorise teaching as a labour process. Writers like Michael Apple have combined the insights of Braverman and Willis. Apple describes how teachers' activities are being rationalised and deskilled; how the curriculum is being increasingly prepackaged according to commercial considerations.[20] Teachers are being forced to teach in ways that are based on behavioural objectives; they are rapidly becoming 'managers' of knowledge who must be accountable and cost effective.

The Gramscian approach

The Gramscian approach is very important because of its insights about education and its understanding of the nature of the advanced industrial nations of the 'West'. Gramsci has helped me to realise that the central organising principle of the school in capitalism is the reproduction of the mental/manual division. He argued that the structural cause of working-class failure lies in the division of mental and manual labour. For most working-class people this brings about not merely a lack of cultural skills and habits necessary for study but an ideology that legitimates failure among working-class people themselves, who have come to accept the division between thinkers (the professional 'experts') and the doers as a natural one.

Gramsci believed that the labour movement should take the lead in education and that it should be provided at the point of production. It was the task of the party to encourage all forms of cultural production by the working class. Education, then, is the cultural preparation for leadership.

Leadership is connected with hegemony. For Gramsci hegemony is to do with economic, political, intellectual, moral leadership.[21] The achievement and maintenance of hegemony is largely a matter of education. A hegemonic class is the class that has the ability to articulate the interests of other social groups to its own by means of ideological struggle. In other words, hegemony is constructed not by domination but with the consent of different groups. It is a consensus resulting from the genuine adoption of the interests of the popular classes by the hegemonic class which gives rise to the creation of a genuine 'national- popular' will. Hegemony is the creation of a 'new common sense'. Politics is about not domination but the creation of a new culture.

Let me now sum up. My argument is this: symbolic interactionism has no notion of the economic base. (And yet, have you noticed that as the crisis deepens the interactionist approach is having a revival?) Humanist marxism has a deep suspicion of the economic base. Bowles and Gintis have a mechanistic view of the base/superstructure which lacks an understanding of contradictions. In structuralist marxism there is an understanding of the base and superstructure and its contradictions but there are difficulties. Is the view that 'the economy is determinate in the last instance' economistic? What does 'in the last instance' mean? And then there is the concept 'relative autonomy'; surely, the levels must either be determined or they are autonomous? Althusser cannot have it both ways. Willis is very critical of Althusser and argues that within the working class there is a creative self-making process which he calls cultural production, but this is treated in isolation from the economic base. I want to know the relationships, the connections, between cultural production and economic production.

13

Though this brief chapter may give the impression that there is a succession of approaches I think there is, rather, a constant re-thinking, re-working, of difficult problems — attempts to focus on different aspects of a complex dynamic social totality. I believe that it is important fully to understand the different approaches I have outlined and their different theorisations of the base/superstructure relationship because these approaches lead to different analyses of schooling and they have different political effects.

One of the main limitations of this chapter and of the classical marxism which it represents is that it focuses only on the class dynamic — it neglects gender and 'race'. I think that marxist feminism has made a vital contribution in the last few years by widening the areas of debate. And now a black marxism is beginning to emerge which is raising new issues. In the next chapter I will consider some of the contradictions between the dynamics of class, gender and 'race' as they relate to black children in schools.

Chapter 2

Class, gender and race: black pupils in schools

Having outlined some of the approaches to education I want to argue that in spite of their great analytical power they tend to neglect the dynamics of gender and 'race'. In this chapter, therefore, I want to consider some of the interrelationships between class, gender and 'race', and link the discussion with the everyday experiences of pupils and teachers.

Class and 'race'

There are many ways of thinking about the relationship between class and 'race'. It was Karl Marx who put class on the political agenda. Before Marx there were many writers who 'made appeals to a 'common humanity', 'common interest' or 'general will', but it was Marx who drew attention to the fact that all history is the history of class struggle — between slave and master, serf and lord, the proletariat and the bourgeoisie. I have already said that the Marxist concept of class has nothing to do with the empirical. The concept of class refers to an objective relationship to the means of production independent of will or attitude. A person's class position strongly conditions consciousness and culture.

In my own work I have always stressed the role of imperialism; basically, capitalist countries have a need for cheap, raw materials and extensive markets for the sale of their commodities. The whole structure of white racism is built on economic exploitation. But it is cemented with white culture: white schools, white law, white politics. And so it is not surprising that many black people feel that they are oppressed by white people. Now, I would argue that behind white 'individuals' lie the *structures* of capital. It is because these structures lie beneath or behind the appearance and cannot be immediately grasped that we need to develop our concepts and refine our theories.

There are many conceptual difficulties in this area. Let me give you just two examples concerning the relationship between gender, class and race: what do you think of the following statement? 'The black man, by virtue of his particular oppression, is closer to his bourgeois brother (by colour) than to his white comrade ... A common experience of racial oppression ... ranges the black worker on the side of the black bourgeois against their common enemy: the white man, worker and bourgeois alike.'[1] Do you think this is true? In the second example let's consider a black, working-class woman: does she suffer from double or treble forms of oppression? Is this a process of aggregation or of complex contradictions within and between each 'dynamic'?

In the political arena blacks are bitterly divided. Some reject left wing radicals and socialist organisations because of their racist practices. Experiencing employers, unions, police, an educational system and a state that are all racist, they feel hostile to the agents and institutions. And so some blacks prioritize race. They believe that the primary political conflict is between the 'black masses' and the racism of an authoritarian state. In short, the struggle of black people is regarded as autonomous and separate — they are not interested in the problems of the white working class (which they often experience as racist).

Other blacks, however, are making alliances with whites and are joining political parties. There are problems in this area also. Some Afro-Caribbeans think of themselves as proletarian and are antagonistic to Asians who they see not as black comrades but as members of a self-employed shopkeeper class, the petit bourgeoisie.

It is very difficult to theorize the precise relationship between class and 'race' in contemporary Britain. Broadly speaking there are four main approaches:

The first approach, associated with Weberian and Marxist analysis, argues that economic relations have a primacy in determining the character of 'race' politics. Weberians tend to see blacks as an 'underclass', whilst Marxists see them as members of the 'sub-proletariat'. For Weberians like John Rex and Sally Tomlinson, an underclass status results from the accumulated effect of losing struggles in the distributive sphere.[2] Blacks fare consistently badly in the market for jobs, housing, education. Racial structuration is imposed by capital but it is compounded and deepened by state agencies which try to regulate the ebb and flow of black labour power in capital's interests. In brief, John Rex emphasizes class (rather than race) and has a Weberian point of view. His position is an example of what has been called the 'liberal' sociology of 'race relations' because it wants to ameliorate the present system rather than change it in any radical way.

In the marxist version of this approach, the term sub-proletariat allows black socialists a means to retain a link with class theory. It encourages activists to open a dialogue with the Left while directing their energies towards the development of relatively autonomous black political activity. The work of Sivanandan is an example of this approach. He has done an enormous amount of work as director of the Institute of Race Relations to encourage and develop the theoretical basis of an anti-racist perspective, and has become increasingly aware of the role of economic factors such as imperialism and multi-national capitalism.[3] Sivanandan emphasizes race and class. He argues that the relationship between racism and capitalism is an instrumental one in which capital requires racism not for racism's sake but for the sake of capital. And so struggles against racism are an integral part of the struggles against capitalism.

The second approach stresses that 'races' do not exist in any biological/scientific sense. This approach, exemplified in the work of Robert Miles, asserts that 'race' is nothing more than an ideological effect. He attacks all writers who use the term 'race' as if it was a scientific category and he is particularly critical of the sociologists of race relations. (I will discuss these points in a moment.) As Miles stresses Marxist political economy and class struggle, he opposes separatist black organisations. Miles writes that there is a complete discontinuity between the interests of the black petit bourgeois and black working-class settlers, but there is always the possibility that fractions of the black petit bourgeois can change sides and make links with the working class. In short, Miles regards the dissolving of 'race' into class as a necessary and desirable step.

In the third approach racism does not appear to have any contact with class politics at all. Some theorists, like J. Gabriel and G. Ben-Tovim, stress the production of critiques of official 'race' policy and the formulation of alternative 'rational policy recommendations' which can facilitate the 'rational political interventions' of central and local governments.[4] In this approach it is assumed that state institutions have the capacity to act as an agent for the elimination of racism. But I would have thought that this cannot be taken for granted. Even where a progressive, radical local authority acts in the name of anti-racism its practices may reinforce the very ideologies it is seeking to challenge.

These approaches are obviously very different. Whilst Miles believes that political conflicts can be addressed by appealing to a fundamental unity of workers based on their common class position, Gabriel and Ben-Tovim see 'race' struggles not as class struggles but as 'popular-democratic'.[5] The latter believe that racism is bad ideology and that it must be combatted by good, popular-democratic, ideology. Race relations legislation, multicultural education policies and racism awareness training are the favoured vehicles for doing this. In the Gabriel and Ben-Tovim approach 'race' becomes merely a policy issue; it loses contact with history and class politics.

In the approaches outlined above 'race' is related to an overarching class structure but many social thinkers nowadays stress not class but the new social movements. They focus on the struggles around gender, sexuality, generation, the consumption and distribution of state services, and ecological and regional conflicts as well as those defined by 'race'. For Paul Gilroy 'these heterogeneous struggles somehow encompass class and are in the process of *moving beyond* the challenge to the mode of production which defines class politics'.[6] There is, then, a fourth approach. Paul Gilroy believes that 'race' can no longer be reduced to an effect of the economic antagonisms arising from production and that class must be understood in terms qualified by the vitality of struggles articulated through 'race'. He argues that 'race' could, perhaps, provide a more effective means of organizing the grievances of inner-city populations than the language of class politics.

I think that the most polemical approach is probably that of Robert Miles. He has some interesting things to say about the concept of 'race' and the sociology of 'race relations'. Let us, therefore, look more deeply at Miles' argument. He contends that race, as it has no scientific validity, is an ideology. *Race does not exist, nevertheless, this commonsense and ideological notion has effects.* In his view the 'black masses' are not a 'race' which has to be related to class, but rather are persons whose forms of political struggle can be understood in terms of racialisation (or racial categorization) within a set of production and class relations.[7]

As race is an ideological concept (there is loud laughter whenever I tell black audiences that race does not exist) it has no analytic value, no explanatory importance. It cannot constitute the object of a general theory. The object of analysis can only be the construction, mobilisation and pertinence of different forms of racist ideology and structuration in specific historical circumstances. As a recognition of this point I will henceforth ask you to read the word race as if it was always in quote marks.

Miles declares that there is both a 'liberal' and a 'radical' sociology of 'race relations', the former approach being exemplified in the work of John Rex, and the latter by Sivanandan and Paul Gilroy, et. al. In his view writers like Gilroy (and Sivanandan) reify race and race relations. These authors, who write in the marxist tradition should not legitimize an ideological notion ('race') by elevating it to a central analytical position.

Turning to the main features of 'race relations' sociology, Miles states that in this perspective the 'black community' or the black masses are often presented as being 'apart from' or 'outside' the working class. This is most explicit in the work of Rex and Tomlinson, and Sivanandan; nevertheless, these writers employ the concept of underclass and/or its synonym, subproletariat in an attempt to retain a link with class analysis. In their writings the black community is depicted as being involved in a struggle against racism but the question of the extent of participation of the 'black masses' in trade unions and in the various parties of the left is not usually discussed. Indeed, the British working class is not considered to have any definite role, primarily because of its role in reproducing racism, but also because of its attributed integration into the benefits of the 'welfare state'.

Another characteristic feature of sociologists of 'race relations' is that they neglect or deny the importance of production relations. They are silent on the question of class divisions within the 'black masses' and on the consciousness and practice of various 'fractions' of the British working class. Even in the 'radical' sociology of 'race relations' little mention is made of the position of 'black people' in *production relations*. This is important because the marxist concept of class refers primarily, but not exclusively, to the location of groups in production relations. The position of 'black' workers in production relations obviously has an effect on their political consciousness.

In many of the texts of the sociology of 'race relations', 'black people', 'black communities' are seen as a collective in opposition to the capitalist state and 'white' society. But we should remember that Asian and Caribbean migrants and their British-born children do not constitute a homogeneous political force as a consequence of racism. There are many differences between Asian and Caribbean cultures. One problem is, after having noted these differences, to what extent should we reaffirm the essential unity of 'black' people? Perhaps we should use the word 'black' as a political category, rather like one uses the word 'red' or 'green'?

Miles draws attention to the fact that black people are to be found not only in the ranks of the reserve army of labour (the unemployed), but also within the proletariat and the petit bourgeoisie. He wants to underline the point that the political class struggle of the various agents occupying these different sites will be directly influenced by their position in (or exclusion from) *production relations*.

He also suggests that insufficient attention has been paid to the 'black' petite-bourgeoisie. This class is important as it is one element of the state's strategy to defuse dissent, to neutralise revolt, by the creation and support for such a class fraction.[8]

Some writers insist that the central determinant of the reproduction of racism is the activity of the state. (This, of course, raises many questions: what is the role of the state? what is the relationship between state and capital?) Miles writes that what we need to know is the relationship between the role of the state and the political ideology and practice of the various fractions of the working class. Obviously, much depends on the role played by the state in the legitimation and reproduction of racism.

For Miles 'a crucial component of the explanation for working-class racism lies with the way in which sections of the working class have themselves interpreted their own experience, in combination with dominant ideas, through the idea of 'race' in order to provide an explanation for their material and political circumstances. But it is also the case that the direct experience of the capital/wage labour relation generates alternative and contradictory conceptions, conceptions which challenge that ideological representation which employs the idea of 'race'.[9] We need an analysis of both the reproduction of racism and the development of anti-racist practice within the working class as a whole.

It has been suggested by Miles that Gilroy, et.al., and Sivanandan retain the ideological notion of 'race' to weld together a population of distinct historical and cultural origins, occupying different class positions, in order to legitimise and encourage the formation of a particular political force. Thus they struggle against racism, but retain and legitimate the idea of 'race' for political reasons. In this process, though they have eradicated the negative connotations of 'race', they are nevertheless legitimating the commonsense understanding of 'race'. They confirm the racial categorization which is the product of practices by the state, the political parties, and within the working class.

In short, Miles sees the class/race dichotomy as a false one. Struggles can be analysed without employing 'race' and 'race relations' as analytical categories. (He acknowledges, however, that the use of these ideological notions in the everyday world and in political analysis requires explanation.) From his perspective 'black' people are racialised class fractions. Though his work is grounded in a class analysis (the political economy of labour migration) he realizes that one of the central political and ideological processes in contemporary capitalist societies is the process of racialisation.

Gender and the politics of feminism

Whatever position we adopt about the relationship between class and 'race' we have at the same time to consider also the dynamic of sex and gender. It is essential to distinguish between sex and gender. The term sex refers to the biological realm and the term gender is associated with the social. The importance of this distinction lies in the fact that what is biological is natural and is hard to change, whilst that which is social — those phenomena created by human beings — is regarded as being changeable. Often we forget that what we think of as 'natural' is really social. Understandably, there are many controversies about exactly what is natural and what is social. The second point is that there are many differences about these matters within the women's movements (note the plural). These differences arise out of different theoretical perspectives.

The main theoretical perspectives on gender inequality are liberal feminist, radical feminist, socialist feminist and black feminist perspectives.[10] To put it briefly, the liberal feminist perspective prioritizes questions of equal access and choice for women. The main criticism of this perspective is that it ignores questions of power. The radical feminist perspective does analyse power, but focuses on the relation between men and women, on patriarchy; it neglects 'class' and 'race'. The socialist feminist perspective emphasizes the fact that women have a dual relationship to the class structure involving a *direct* relation of exploitation by capital with respect to a woman's position as a wage labourer, and an *indirect one* in so far as many women depend upon the mediated wage of a male breadwinner. Sadly, all these perspectives have little to say about the experience of black women; on questions of racism they remain silent.

Many interesting and important debates are taking place between radical feminists and socialist feminists. Radical feminists believe that their enemy is not capital but patriarchy — the rule of men and/or the dominance of male values. Many radical feminists are lesbians and believe in an autonomous, segregated movement; they are separatists. Socialist feminists believe that the main enemy is (not patriarchy but) capitalism. Men are implicated, but usually they are agents of capital rather than the source of exploitation. They are against autonomous movements and believe that men and women must learn to live and struggle together on equal terms (though consciousness raising may have to be done separately for a limited period).

The main question, then, is: from what source does oppression arise? Does it arise from domination by capital, by patriarchy, or by white power? Or some interrelation of these forces? This is an important question because we may want to know, at a particular time, which struggle should be prioritized.

There may be occasions when struggles come together; at other times the 'dynamics' of race, sex and class may oppose each other and result in contradictions.

During the last few years many women have begun to feel that marxism neglects questions of subjectivity and sexuality and so have become interested in psychoanalysis. The work of Sigmund Freud and Jacques Lacan, for example, has been popularized by Rosalind Coward, Juliet Mitchell and many others.[11] Socialist feminists have made a considerable contribution to the study of education. I am thinking of the work of Madeleine Arnot, Miriam David, Rosemary Deem, Rachel Sharp, Ann Marie Wolpe and others. These writers are interested in the employment market, the role of the family, the socialization of girls — and boys.

As an example of the different approaches adopted by the radical feminists and the socialist feminists let us consider for a moment the issue of whether girls receive a better education in single sex or co-educational schools. Most socialist feminists support (comprehensive) co-educational schools. ('After all, to eradicate sexism, it is the thinking of boys that has to be changed.') Radical feminists and Muslims, however, are against such schools. They support single sex schools — but for different reasons. Muslims believe that females should be schooled separately from males; radical feminists argue that in single sex schools there is more chance for girls to develop themselves, there is a wider range of role models and that educational achievement is higher. Though radical feminists and Muslims are campaigning for segregated schools, the contradiction is that most white feminist groups believe that Islam is sexist.

Until recently white feminists ignored the question of racism altogether. They failed to address the problems of black women. Much of feminist theory is based on a narrow, white, middle-class model of womanhood, and its basic assumptions are Eurocentric.[12] As feminist theory incorporated many of the racist assumptions inherent in our society, most black women regarded it as irrelevant — even racist. It was felt that white women, even if aware of their oppression by men, are equally responsible for the oppression of black people.

The black feminist perspective is highly critical of Western feminist thought because of its ethnocentricity. The latter assumes that 'Third World' societies are 'traditional' and 'superstitious', whilst First World societies are 'progressive' and 'civilized'. Too often Western feminism serves to reproduce rather than challenge the categories through which 'the West' constructs itself as superior to other peoples. The black feminist perspective rightly castigates Western scholarship because of the way it categorizes 'non-

Western' people as Other. It will be argued in chapter 6 of this book that, in constructing the Other as marginal or pathological, Western scholarship has a hegemonic role in global and political struggles. In recent years the imposition of Western 'norms' on the rest of the world has been increasingly questioned. There is a growth in the movement which asks of the West 'what entitles its culture, its science, its social organisation, and finally its rationality itself, to be able to claim universal validity: was this not a mirage associated with economic domination and political hegemony?'[13] This theme will be explored in a later chapter on imperialism.

I willingly concede that marxism has neglected the discussion of many topics such as the family, sexuality, women's history. It is probably true that the social domination of men over women predates capital. Sexual domination is so much older historically, and more deeply rooted culturally as a pattern of inequality, than class exploitation. But it has to be acknowledged that there is no specialized agency for the repression of women. This may mean that there is little possibility of unity amongst women as there is no totalized adversary. It is for this reason that I would agree with those thinkers who suggest that the women's movements do not have the leverage to transform capital.[14] Without the supersession or abolition of classes there is small chance of the equalization of the sexes. This seems to me as obvious as saying that without the dismantling of capital there is little likelihood of the banishment of nuclear war.

I have been critical of radical feminism because I think that it is a bourgeois movement. Radical feminists want the same opportunities as men; this is fair enough but they are more interested in increasing their own life chances rather than trying to change the economic system. In many areas such as nuclear science and war research, for example, men are dominant. Now radical feminists want the same opportunities as men, but I don't want more people in these industries even if they are women. I would prefer such industries to come under democratic control and be made accountable. In short, radical feminists want more power but in doing so they often support the capitalist structure of society rather than challenge it.

For similar reasons I am against separatist (or autonomous) 'black' organisations. Scientifically speaking, 'race' does not exist — yet its effects, racism, exists. I think people should think of themselves not as members of a 'race' but of a class. Blacks and whites, men and women have to learn to work together; whites have to become more aware of 'race', blacks have to become more aware of class.

Many socialist feminists have always recognized that most black people are 'objectively' members of the working class. Radical feminists, I repeat, focus on not capital but patriarchy as the source of oppression. In the last few years, however, an important change has occurred: many radical feminists, working on 'equal opportunities' programmes and policies, have been forced to consider the question of racial discrimination. In the field of education, for example, some white feminists are now saying that it is impossible to develop anti-sexist strategies for all pupils without considering also how racism enters the school.

Black pupils in school

I now want to link the discussion about class, gender and 'race' to the problem of racism in schools. Black children experience racism from teachers, from other pupils, and through the overt and covert curriculum. Many schools are at fault because they do not recognize the needs of their black pupils. Since the 1970s it has constantly been said that black pupils have a negative self-image and that this accounts for their under-achievement in schools. I think that this psychological view has become a sort of 'commonsense', and that it distracts attention from institutional racism.

It is not true that all black pupils underachieve. Indian pupils perform better than those from Pakistan and Bangladesh, and these groups perform better than Afro-Caribbeans. How do we explain these astonishing differences? Is it to do with class? Is it significant that though most black people live in inner, urban cities, it is the Asians that have the greater cultural cohesion?

Let us now look at some 'facts' about the educational performance of black pupils which I think are very interesting and which raise many questions. It may be a useful exercise for you to try and 'explain' the following findings.

1   The length of stay in this country seemed important in terms of increased performance. Pupils who came to England before the age of eight attained higher reading scores.

2   It has been found that sixteen year old pupils from ethnic minority groups who were born in this country to immigrant parents in general performed considerably better in reading and mathematics than did those who were themselves immigrants.

3   When the researchers examined the average performances of different ethnic groups, however, they found that, in mathematics, only the mean scores for the Irish and the West Indians were below the average of all groups. The pupils of West Indian origin alone were below average in reading.

4   Pupils from West Indian origin families achieve fewer higher grades in English and mathematics than either their Asian or white peers. Asian pupils performed slightly better than both groups in mathematics. When examination performance in all subjects was looked at, it was found that the Asian success was not limited to mathematics but was reflected in a higher proportion of Asians gaining five or more CSE 1 or O level grade A — C awards. Similarly, the proportion of Asians gaining at least an A level pass was also slightly higher than for both other groups.[15]

5   It is quite clear that both Asians and West Indians use further education more than their peers. Despite the fact that West Indian and Bengali (Bangladeshi) pupils still underachieve, some studies indicate a continued rise in the education performance and opportunity of black pupils as a whole.[16]

6   The most striking finding is the fact that a half of Asian young women have no qualifications, vocational or academic, compared with only a fifth of white and West Indian young women. However, the proportion with A levels and degrees is similar for Asians and whites, suggesting a polarization between young Asian women with good academic qualifications and those with none at all. There is also evidence that this situation is rapidly changing, with many more Asian women gaining academic qualifications.

7   Black men and women are more likely to extend their education beyond the minimum school-leaving age than white men and women. This is particularly true of Asian men and women and West Indian women.

An interesting finding is that some black girls who were doing well at school suddenly started doing badly. It has been suggested that this might happen because many schools ignore the development of girls' sexuality. This lack of validation is one reason why many youngsters want to leave school altogether. A blunt, shorthand way of saying this is: 'school is boring'.

As students and teachers, it is imperative that we consider the following questions: what are the forces at work which lead to the absence of black pupils in some schools and their presence in others? Why is there an absence of black teachers? What does the status or complete absence of black teachers in the schools mean in terms of role models for black pupils and white?

We also need to think about how racism shapes the experiences of black pupils. How do we break down forms of institutional racism in, for example, the allocation of black female pupils in lower ability streams, their routing into non-examination courses, their separation into English as a Second Language (ESL) classes, and the prevalent expectation that their future lives only require domestic training and child care?

These are complex and difficult questions, partly because young black women's experiences of living in a racist society are determined by many factors such as race, gender, age, class, religion and sexuality. It is clear, however, that there is a pervasive pathologising of Asian cultures and Asian family structures. Many teachers I have talked to think that the main problems with their pupils arise from strict parental attitudes. Young Asian women are wrongly stereotyped as meek, mild and docile. White teachers often believe that Asian students will be victims of forced arranged marriages. This has often resulted in young women being denied adequate career counselling. It is important for teachers to realize that work with Asian girls cannot be developed in isolation from their families and communities. It is essential for parents to be consulted and their trust gained.[17]

Contradictions

It is often assumed that racism, patriarchy and class exploitation operate in similar ways and reinforce one another. The constant reiteration that teachers must be aware of gender, race and class inequalities leads many of them to think that methods developed in one context can be applied to parallel initiatives in other areas. But an advance in, say, anti-sexist education does not necessarily mean an advance in anti-racist education. The relationships between the dynamics of gender, class and race are not fixed, and the relationships between them are continually shifting, producing uneven and indeed contradictory effects.

Consider some of the everyday experiences of teaching in a multi- ethnic, co-educational school. If a black teacher disciplines a white pupil for a racist remark, that action may imply that the black community, which the teacher represents, will not tolerate racial abuse. But if the teacher happens to be a woman and the pupil is male, the same act may be interpreted in a different way, as that of a mother 'telling off' a naughty child. This may provoke a patriarchal rather than a racist response. If the anti-racist teacher is white the intervention is much more likely to be decoded by the pupil in class terms and the teacher will be seen as one of 'them' that side with the blacks against 'us'.

If anti-sexist education is taught in a heavy-handed manner black boys and white may form a coalition and retaliate by celebrating 'macho' values. On the other hand, the shared experience of boys' sexism may bring black girls and white together, and this alliance may shift the latter's attitude on race. Sometimes the sexual 'double standard' may get translated into a racial one, in which Afro-Caribbean cultures are positively associated with masculine and proletarian values, whereas Asian cultures are despised as 'effeminate' and 'petit-bourgeois'.

Writers like Phil Cohen, Paul Corrigan, Paul Willis and others have drawn our attention to the many white working-class pupils who resist authority through school counter-culture. Recent research shows that the 'guerrilla warfare' which is waged against classroom discipline is now often linked with racist practices. Usually most pupils play it cool; they give an outward display of conformity, refraining from making racist remarks in the classroom whilst inwardly maintaining a racist position, which is then openly expressed as soon as the teacher's back is turned. There are also some pupils who deliberately 'wind up' a teacher in order to provoke a response. About such a situation Cohen has written: 'If the teacher treats it seriously as a disciplinary matter, then s/he is shown up as someone who can't take a joke. If s/he ignores it, then the pupil has got away with it.'[18]

The phenomenon of split perception is also well known. This is when an individual makes a personal or cultural exception to his or her racist beliefs: 'Pakis stink but Ahmed is alright, he's my friend.' Some pupils, usually those with a middle-class orientation, tend to adopt a *laissez faire* attitude. They show tolerance because none of their privileges are threatened. But even when relations between black pupils and white are relatively trouble free there may be a displacement effect. In some schools, for example, there is racist banter between Afro-Caribbean and Asian pupils. There are many cases of divisions within and between ethnic communities, divisions which are encouraged by the state and its agencies. The ideology of ethnicity is often used to divide and fragment black people.

There are, then, many strategies of racist disavowal including silent racism. What is worrying is this: we know that many working-class pupils are deeply alienated from the education system, and we also know that racism is strong in many working-class areas. There is now a danger that *racism may become another way of expressing an anti-school position*, which is then reinforced by certain types of youth culture.

But it is not only the pupils that are racist; I regret to say that there are still many racist teachers. Black kids are difficult to teach, they say. 'If they are going to live here they should learn to adapt to the British way of life.' A common charge now is that the implementation of anti-racist policies means that white pupils are being put at a disadvantage. Many teachers are middle class and their privileges enable them to adopt a 'liberal' attitude which is actually patronising, hypocritical and often ignorant. Perhaps any white person growing up in a racist society such as Britain is inevitably going to hold some racist views. This is largely because of the residues of imperialism, the sense of superiority acquired during the days of the Raj. In this section I have tried to signal the fact that racism is a difficult problem to overcome. It can be silenced in one context only to reappear in an even more virulent form in another. What, then, is the most effective approach to adopt?

Chapter 3

Multicultural and/or antiracist education?

Multicultural education

The other day I went to visit one of my students on teaching practice in a school in east London, a part of the city where many immigrants live. No, I should not use that word anymore, I must remember that most of the children were born here; they are not immigrants but black British. I observed a delightful drama lesson and then I suddenly noticed that there were no black children in the class. I asked why. She replied, 'They burn them out'. I understood. She did not have to explain to me that in this particular part of London there are no Asian families because if they move into the area, petrol is poured in through their letter boxes at night and their homes set on fire.

Many readers will be aware that there is a bitter controversy about whether the most effective response to racism is multicultural and/or anti-racist education. I think this debate amongst teachers and educationalists, parents and politicians is a political issue — it is actually an ideological struggle about the type of society in which we want to live.

During the early 1970s it was increasingly realized that neither assimilation nor integration was working. Teachers saw that these approaches were both patronizing and dismissive of other cultures. In reaction to these ethnocentric approaches there was a move towards 'cultural pluralism'. In education this trend is called multicultural education.

In this approach many teachers stress the importance of direct experiential learning about other cultures. It is said that teaching about other people's cultures promotes a positive 'self- image' amongst black people who suffer from a 'poor self-concept'. The emphasis is on breaking down stereotypes and promoting greater tolerance of diversity in society.

Let me give a typical example. Recently I visited an east London school to see an exhibition of objects — cooking pots and utensils, toys and fans, saris and wall plaques — produced by Bangladeshi villagers for their everyday use. Also on display were some paintings based on the above resources done by local school children. One of the (white) art teachers explained his 'multicultural' approach to me. I found myself admiring the still-life paintings of these objects which were all done in the European tradition of still-life painting. In his artroom new objects had been introduced (Chinese last term, African the next), removed from their context and transformed into exotica. Art for art's sake. An anti-racist teacher would, I think, be more fully informed about not only the artistic, but also the historical, sociological and political background of these objects, and would impart an understanding of their production, usage and value in the context of the culture that produced them.

In the many schools I have visited multicultural education largely consists of looking at the quaintness of other people's cultural habits, their food, clothes and music. I have argued against this approach, in a previous book, because it focuses on life *styles* — the appreciation of other cultures — and not on political processes and economic structures.

Most liberal individualists and social democrats are in the multicultural camp. They tend to stress personal attitudes rather than social forces. They see multiculturalism, basically, as a plea for toleration, and do not really want to challenge the present dominance of the ethnocentric paradigm. They want to devise effective ways of evolving a non-racist education system — but one which does not challenge the status quo. Not wishing to challenge the capitalist system in any way, they accuse antiracist teachers of having ('blatant') political objectives. Much of this 'soft' multicultural education, then, is tokenistic, but it is more than that; as it is involved in an ideological struggle it actually tries to prevent radical social change. There is some evidence that this 'liberal-experiential' approach is proving unproductive, and in recent years, a powerful critique has been mounted against it.

Criticisms of multicultural education

Multicultural education has been attacked from both the political Right and the Left. Before I outline the criticisms from the Left, let me quickly sketch the right wing view. Fundamentally, right wing critics believe that black people should be integrated into British society. A teacher's job is to treat all children alike and, as all pupils are the same, no attention must be paid to 'racial' and cultural differences. In their view most problems are caused by extremist blacks who don't appreciate what Britain has done for them. It may be counter-productive to improve race relations too fast. It is important that the curriculum of British schools should reflect British traditions, history and culture. ('And if they don't like it, why don't they go back?') A characteristic feature of right wing ideologues is that any criticism of British, capitalist society is immediately seen as a sign of the rejection of British traditions and values. I find that most right wing critics are rather arrogant; they take it for granted that they have nothing to learn from black people. When they attack multicultural education most of their underlying assumptions are clearly those associated with the discredited assimilationist approach. I will return to this topic in a later section.

Let me now enumerate some of the criticisms of multicultural education from the Left. Some writers have argued that the introduction of 'multicultural' elements into the teaching of black children is an irrelevance based on the erroneous view that black children have a poor self-image, and that it deflects from the need to teach normal basic skills effectively. 'Multicultural' education ('lots of steel bands and sports') thus adversely affects the education of black children; it is a misguided liberal strategy to compensate black children for not being white.[1]

Many supporters of multicultural education see racism as a set of mental *prejudices* held by a small number of unenlightened white people. They therefore deny the *structural* aspects of racism both in society and in the education system. Multicultural education focuses only on culture; moreover it reflects a *white* view of black cultures as homogeneous, static and conflict-free. It is preoccupied with exotic aspects of cultural difference and ignores the effects of racism. After all, just to learn about other people's cultures is not to learn about the racism of one's own.

Multicultural education ignores issues such as the economic position of black people in relation to white people; differences in access to resources; discrimination in employment, housing and education; relations with the police. This approach disregards the issue of racism.

Multiculturalism excludes discussion of power; it takes no note of the power relations between white people and black, both past and present. It also takes no account of the forms of resistance to the dominant power bloc. Indeed some black writers believe that multiculturalism is a conscious strategy to contain the challenge presented by disaffected black youth. Multicultural education, in brief, is a sophisticated form of social control and it has the effect of keeping black resistance in check. Its aim is to prevent basic changes in the power structure of society.

How can I best sum up the significance, the 'essence', of multicultural education? I think that the main values and beliefs underlying multiculturalism are expressed in the following passage. James Lynch in an article on 'The Multicultural Curriculum' writes:

> 'I suppose what I am proposing is similar to the process of delivering people from intellectual, moral and spiritual bondage which education represents for many at the moment, and of recognizing education, as Stenhouse (1978) argues, as the potential instrument of a redistribution of the means of autonomy and judgment. The right to judgment is redistributed as is the autonomy to feel in a position to formulate tentative judgments subject to critical public appraisal.'[2]

Notice that reference is made to 'delivering people from intellectual, moral and spiritual bondage' but no reference is made to the economic exploitation and domination that so many people in the world suffer from. It is typical of liberal educators like Stenhouse and Lynch that for them the most serious problem with which education has to deal is the 'redistribution of the means of autonomy and judgement'. Supporters of multicultural education always tend to see education in an idealist way; they use the tired phraseology of the liberal philosophy of education so that issues of inequality and injustice are never raised. In their discourse power remains an absent concept.

We should remember that though supporters of multicultural education like Lynch see education as an 'instrument of a *redistribution* of the means of autonomy and judgement', for many people in the freedom movements around the world education is an instrument for the construction of a new society, where what is important is not the redistribution of some idealist and philosophical attributes of the individual person but the establishment of a new society based on the common ownership of the means of *production*, distribution and exchange.

Anti-racist education

Greater awareness of the shortcomings and deficiencies of multicultural education has led to the development of new approaches which emphasize equality and justice. This takes two forms. The 'liberal' approach is that of supporting 'equal opportunities'. The aim of this approach is to remove discrimination based on class, sex, or race. It is liberal in the sense that it wants to improve the 'life-chances' of groups. The problem is that many supporters of 'equal opportunities' want to improve their own life chances but are not at all interested in changing society — they have no critique of capitalism. The second approach, which goes beyond 'liberal' equal opportunities, is called anti-racist education.

In my view anti-racist education suggests that society or the social formation, as it is sometimes called, should be thought of as consisting of a number of distinct interrelated 'levels' of practical activity. The social formation is complex, made up of the economic, the political, ideological and theoretical levels. These levels are determining and determined; there is 'relative autonomy' between and within the levels. In this conception of the social formation there is no necessary correspondence between the three levels; there are, in fact, contradictions within and between levels. Though this conception of the social formation can be criticized, I think you will find it a useful schema to begin thinking about certain problems.

Some writers, like Ellis Cashmore and Barry Troyna, make a distinction between racialism and racism.[3] Racialism is defined as action based on a notion of racial inequality; racism is the theoretical basis of, or justification for, racialist behaviour. To put it another way: racialism refers to practices and racism refers to beliefs. I am critical of this distinction because it separates thought and action, theory and practice. Surely all practice is based on some theory (whether it is conscious or not) and that theory — our ideas and assumptions — cannot be separated from what we do?

I wish to argue that racism should be seen in terms of 'levels', each level containing economic, political and ideological elements. Anti-racist education encourages the analysis of racism on the inter-personal, institutional, state and international 'levels'. *Interpersonal racism* is the racism that occurs between individuals. This is largely the realm of the social psychologist and includes the understanding of personal bias, prejudice, stereotyping and so forth.[4] Interpersonal racism can be conscious or unconscious, that is to say, intentional or unintentional. Many people spend a lot of time discussing whether some racist act was intentional or not. It seems to me that if the effect of the act is racist it doesn't matter very much if it was intentional or unintentional. (In any case unconscious racism cannot be easily explored because it is unconscious.) Sadly, some of the discussions of racism at this inter-personal level seem to be rather limited. They are often a delaying tactic. I would argue that many psychologists reduce conflict to 'inter-group tensions' and ignore social and economic causes. To put it in another way: the stress on the individual level implies that there must be a change at a psychological level — and changes in individual consciousness take a long time. The focus on personal change means that confronting the issue of social change is avoided.

I am critical of many psychological and social-psychological theories because they pathologise black families. Most of these theories exclude black people when 'normal' processes are being studied, yet feature them when pathological or deviant situations are under investigation. This 'normalised absence and pathologised presence' is a powerful dynamic in the construction of racist ideologies.

I must emphasize that in spite of these critical remarks, anti-racist education recognizes the importance of interpersonal racism, it includes an understanding of individual psychology but then goes on to examine *institutional racism*. This is the racism between the levels of the individual and the state, that is to say, the racism manifested in large organisations and institutions such as the trade unions, the legal and medical professions, and so on. Racism, on this level, is often expressed in certain taken-for-granted customs, routine practices and procedures. A national curriculum, constructed without consultation with the 'ethnic minorities', would be an example, I believe, of institutional racism.

At one time I used to think that stereotyping was an aspect of interpersonal racism. I did not fully understand the processes by which stereotypes are taken up and adopted by institutions. In other words, interpersonal and institutional racism are not separate and distinct levels; there are dialectical links between them. Afro-Caribbeans, for example, are stereotyped as being (by nature) colourful, happy-go-lucky, rhythmic and amoral. It is said that Afro-Caribbean people lack a whole culture, that their family life lacks cohesion, that they have 'psychological wounds going back to slavery', and so on. But it is not only individuals and race relations experts but also the media, the police and the state that ascribe certain qualities to young blacks. They have weak family units, language disabilities and unrealistic aspirations. There is talk of psychological maladjustment, cultural conflict and 'cycles of deprivation'. These immutable collective qualities are then transformed into taken-for-granted notions by policy makers and officials in institutions and control agencies.

It is a short step from this to the notion that 'ethnic' or 'minority cultures' are deficient in relation to the dominant culture, and that they need to be remedied through the intervention of the state. In my view the multicultural approach with its focus on the individual rather than the social (the idea that problems lie within the person rather than in society), perpetuates the belief that black people have deficiencies that need compensation. Thus the inadequacies of British society, its institutional and state racism escape examination.

Thirdly, there is state racism. Many people find this difficult to understand as they assume that the state is neutral, as if it were an umpire or a referee. The state is often thought of as being above the struggles of competing groups whose task is to see that justice is done. Because so many people assume that the state must be neutral it is difficult for them to realize that the state can be racist. A well known example is the British immigration law which treats blacks differently from whites.[5] By imposing steadily tighter controls on black immigration, the state appears to have not only acted in a racially discriminatory way but also to have reinforced racist attitudes in the electorate. Many people believe that racism is now built into the mechanisms of the state, and that state racism permeates every aspect of social life.

Fourthly, there is *international racism*. From a system in which labour moved to the centres of capital, imperialism has developed into a world-wide system in which capital moves to wherever there is cheap labour. The new industrial revolution, accelerated by micro-electronics, is based on the exploitation of workers in the peripheries. I would want to argue that the multinational corporations are not only (economically) exploitative, but that they are also racist, they oppress the workers of the so-called 'Third World'.

Anti-racists argue that teachers' use of the multicultural approach, with its emphasis on interpersonal relations, the authentic experience of the individual, and a narrow focus on culture, leads to a persistent neglect of the particular character and force of economic relations. There is a tendency to ignore external determinations. Supporters of multicultural education do not sufficiently realize that social relations are *structured*, that they have a tendency or force of their own and operate, in part, 'behind our backs'.

One of the assumptions of anti-racist education is that the real is a multi-layered structure, consisting of entities and processes lying at different levels of that structure. The empirical world with which we are familiar is on the surface level but is causally connected to 'deeper', ontological levels, and it is by virtue of these causal connections that we can use sense-data, experience and observation in constructing knowledge of the structures and processes of the real. These causal connections cannot themselves be understood through experience, because neither the underlying structures nor the connection between these structures and the empirical world are themselves experienced. The connection can only be reconstructed in knowledge.[6]

In short, anti-racist teachers believe that trying to change people's attitudes is not enough. 'Of course', they say, 'we have to change people's consciousness, but we have to change educational and social structures as well'. They see multicultural education as part of the capitalist state's strategy to defuse black resistance, and antiracist education as being fundamentally about the reallocation of power.

Criticisms of anti-racist education

Let me now outline some of the criticisms that are being made of anti-racist education. One of the leading critics of anti-racist education is Robert Jeffcoate. According to Jeffcoate anti-racism as a 'self-conscious educational ideology' first emerged in the 1970s and it marked itself off from 'the liberal tradition of teaching about race relations'.[7]

He suggests that ethnocentric syllabuses in literature, geography and history are not necessarily racist. They could be a reflection of parochialism, teacher ignorance or sheer curriculum inertia — they could not possibly be an example of institutional racism. He also contends that the congregation of black pupils in bottom streams or sets could not be the result of institutional racism. He writes: 'Working class pupils have long been shown to 'percolate downwards' through streaming and setting systems. As most black people are working class, their position could simply be a more visible representation of this long- standing tendency.'[8] I find this argument unsound. It was found in 1972 that 4.9 per cent of all children in ESN schools were of West Indian origin whereas they constituted 1.1 per cent of the total school population. The official 'explanation' mentioned difficulties with discipline, dialect and teachers' assessments as factors in the over-representation of children of West Indian origin.[9] Surely the complaint is that a disproportionate percentage of black youth are pushed into these places not because of their low ability or their 'educational subnormality' but because they are difficult to 'manage'. I want to suggest that the so-called 'disruptive' behaviour of some black students should, perhaps, be seen as an attempt to create an identity based on resistance to the alienating forces in school and society. One sad, perplexing aspect of this problem is the fact that some working-class children, alienated from school values, often see anti-racist education as just another set of institutional rules.

Jeffcoate also argues against those who complain of the racism of white pupils. He quotes a Home Office report: 'The criminality of youthful hooliganism has worn many different fashions over the past twenty years and combating one particular fashion will not necessarily tackle the violence which uses racialism as the present means through which to express it.' Jeffcoate then comments (note how the question of racism is displaced to another issue, and how racial attacks are made incidental!): 'The Home Office report makes the important point that it is in a sense incidental, for even if there were no ethnic minorities in Britain or racialist organisations to latch on to, these boys would still constitute a problem.'[10]

Like many right wing writers on education, Jeffcoate believes that anti-racists have misidentified the nature of the problem because of their preoccupation with racism to their exclusion of all else, and with outcomes and effects rather than intentions or causation. No wonder, then, that whenever there is an example of discrimination he is always keen to show, if he can, that the behaviour was not necessarily racist. Secondly, he ignores issues of political power and yet at the same time is critical of those who are aware of these realities. Jeffcoate accepts the existence of prejudices and stereotypes, what I would call interpersonal racism, but he rejects the concept of institutional racism.[11] Institutional racism, you may remember, refers to those routine practices, customs and procedures that are maintained by relations and structures of power. Jeffcoate says that he does not find it a useful or valid concept.

Jeffcoate asserts that anti-racists appear to lose faith in normal democratic practice when it comes to engaging with racist opinions and beliefs. He discusses an incident in a classroom in which a fourth year boy says: 'Sir, I think black people should be sent home because this country is overcrowded.' Jeffcoate does not find this unacceptable. His sympathies lie with the Stenhouse approach which emphasized that the classroom is precisely the place where adolescents should be encouraged to express and explore opinions on controversial issues such as 'race' and immigration. In Jeffcoate's view pupils should feel free to express their opinions in the classroom, no matter what their political or ideological content may be, learning at the same time to test them out against publicly accredited criteria of truth and rationality and observe the rule of democratic procedure.

Jeffcoate finds illiberalism everywhere; it is a feature of guidelines and policy documents; of racism awareness workshops because their conclusions are unmistakably foregone; of and in the evaluation of school textbooks and children's literature. The fact that many authorities and schools believe that racist literature should be confiscated is seen by Jeffcoate as a threat to democracy.

Jeffcoate believes that when the committed teacher is of an overtly socialist kind the result is indoctrination (someone taking advantage of a privileged role to influence those under his charge in a manner which is likely to distort their ability to assess the evidence on its own merit). But I would like to raise the question: is this not what capitalist institutions, like the media, are doing all the time? It seems that when conservative teachers and independent schools overtly teach their values, their teaching is not questioned but that when socialists teach — it is indoctrination.

From my reading of Jeffcoate's work he actually seems to think that we live in a democratic society. Many blacks do not believe this. Jeffcoate wants to foster democracy and I admire this but I do wish he would write a little more about the injustice that pervades the lives of black people. He concludes his work with a quotation from a psychologist: 'We learn to respect each other's individuality not by hearing about tolerance, or reading about tolerance or even discussing tolerance but by being tolerated by others and being tolerant in return.[12] Black British people, many of whom were born here, do not want other people's toleration. Many blacks have begun to realise that they do not want tolerance, sympathetic understanding or 'harmony'. Mutual respect between cultures is not enough. Blacks want equality and justice. However, whenever black people express this demand, the state denies the existence of racial discrimination (a move rather like Jeffcoate's), and converts the demand into a need. Thus a political challenge becomes transformed into an inadequacy.

I am familiar with most of the arguments used by the New Right against the advocates of anti-racist education because I have scrutinized their comments on my own work. I have, for example, been criticized for foolishly trying to apply a marxist viewpoint to racism because I should know that 'Karl Marx was probably the most spectacularly anti black racist of all time — though Engels ran him pretty close'.[13] This is rather like attacking liberalism by criticizing the personal misdemeanours of Gladstone.

More seriously, any criticism of racial discrimination and injustice is seen as an attack on Britain, on British values, British traditions, 'our' way of life: 'He can see nothing good in anything British. Our traditions, institutions and view of the world are all condemned as imperialist, racist or, slightly less culpable, reformist.' Advocates of anti-racist education are 'bitter, anti-British ideologues.' It seems to me that conservative critics don't realize that the connotations and resonances attached to the term British vary. Many chauvinist organisations, for example, use the term to imply an exclusion of black people.

According to the conservative critics not only do the anti-racists' arguments lack intellectual detachment but they make 'no attempt to engage in that essential struggle to distinguish between education and indoctrination which all genuine academics accept as a pre-requisite of their calling.' What saddens me is how there is a complete incomprehension on the part of the conservatives to the thoughts and feelings of blacks who have no chance to be heard at all. The widespread evidence of the institutional racism of the police, for example, is totally ignored.

Socialists are often slated for being so utopian that they never make any concrete proposals. And so in *The Politics of Multiracial Education* I made a few suggestions concerning teachers. I wrote that: 1. More black people should be encouraged to enter the teaching service. 2. No white person who is racist should be allowed to enter the teaching professions. 3. All teacher training should include courses on multiracial education. 4. Those teachers that behave in a racist way should be disciplined and their acts considered legal offences. Of course I realized that there were enormous difficulties blocking the way but I did not expect these proposals to be ridiculed by reviewers. After all, they were only the same recommendations that Lord Scarman wanted to be implemented (but which were rejected) by the police force in Britain. Why, I wonder, is the Right so worried about the issue of anti-racist education?

I now want to discuss several criticisms of anti-racist education that I think come from a 'liberal' position. The three main criticisms of anti-racism, *as it is widely practised*, are these: Firstly, it is said that anti-racist education ignores social class. This leads to a tendency to attribute discrimination to racism and sexism even where class is the central issue. And this means that the grievances of the white working class majority are not addressed.

You will have noticed that anti-racist education, as I have defined it, does not ignore social class but stresses its importance. I have to admit, however, that there are differences within the anti-racist movement between the supporters of the 'class and race' position who emphasize class analysis (see, for example, the seminal work of A. Sivanandan and the Institute of Race Relations) and others who uphold the 'race (and class)' position. There are many reasons why the latter do not privilege class. Some do not use the concept of class because they see it as inadequate to deal with the dynamics of race and gender. Some are pragmatic and do not use it because it is a marxist concept or because, they say, it leads to reductionism or essentialism. And there are other reasons also. I believe we should always see class, gender and race as being, in some way, interconnected, but I think that, as yet, no integrated theory of class, gender and race exists.

The second criticism of anti-racism is that it has encouraged aspiring, middle class blacks to play the 'skin game' with the collusion of liberal whites. A few unrepresentative blacks have been put into positions of false power, a form of tokenism, without in any way empowering the black population.

It is true that many aspiring middle class blacks have done well out of the 'race industry' as it is called but the anti-racist movement can hardly be blamed for that. The phenomenon of getting on in the system, of 'making it', is common amongst the white working class also. This strategy of incorporation is well known — it is a process actively encouraged by the ruling class. There is an aspect of this question which is a genuine dilemma in political life. Members of oppressed groups often face the choice of getting *something* done, however little, which leads them towards reformism and compromise with the establishment, or of remaining outside conventional, reformist politics, pure but powerless.

The third criticism of anti-racism is that it treats all whites as racist. It is often said that anti-racism has reinforced the guilt of many whites and paralysed them when any issue of race arises. It has taught others to bury their racism without in any way changing their attitude. It has led to resentment and stopped free discussion.

Anti-racist teachers and educators make the point that whites do profit, in different ways, from capitalist exploitation of the 'Third World', that all imperialist countries have profited from their Empires. It is difficult for whites to escape from that socialization which inculcated and justified their imperial role. British culture is saturated with feelings of cultural superiority, attitudes deriving from their 'civilizing mission'. Now, anti-racist education does try to make all people aware of aspects of history which have remained hidden.

If people have buried their racism without in any way changing their attitude this is not because 'anti-racist education is a disaster' (a common phrase in the media) but because it has sometimes been ineffectively taught. This is exactly what happens on anti-sexist courses too. Sexists often say they feel that the free expression of their views has been curtailed!

Conclusion

Many teachers have tried hard to replace stereotypes with positive images and alternative hero/ines. Though a few have done good work, some teachers have not been successful because they have an undialectical view of gender, 'race' and class. They do not realize that they are not homologous structures and that *to undermine one is not necessarily to weaken the others.* There is no fixed or direct principle of correspondence. The methods which are effective in one sphere cannot be used in the same way elsewhere.

Many teachers involved in multicultural education, as Philip Cohen has shown, have a deficit view of working class culture.[14] They often see middle class culture as a haven of tolerance and understanding. Teaching against racism all too easily becomes a part of the traditional burden of trying to 'civilize' the working class.

Moreover, many teachers think that racism can be eradicated by overcoming false ideas by replacing them with correct ones, by giving the true, historical facts about imperialism, or the real reasons for immigration.[15] This could be called the 'elightenment model' of anti-racist work.

Now one of the criticisms of this view is that it assumes that racism is a false belief system and that it can be dealt with by the application of a superior logic. But, as many social scientists have pointed out, racism does not work in this way, it is not a form of logic but a way of 'making sense'. Indeed, the ideological unity of a discourse is perfectly compatible with a wide margin of logical inconsistency.[16] In other words, reasoned argument based on facts and logic is not enough. This kind of rationalist pedagogy is inadequate because many forms of racism are impervious to reason. Teachers may demonstrate that racist arguments are nonsense in the classroom but this does not necessarily lessen the appeal of conspiracy theories as a source of myth and fantasy acted out in the streets and on the football terraces.

I would like to make another point about challenging stereotypes. The question of the representation of black people brings us back again to the problematic relationship between class and race. Most teaching strategies seek to promote a positive image of black people and to prohibit negative images but the problem is that there is a wide divergence of opinion about this. What constitutes a positive or negative image of black people? On the one hand, many teachers prefer images of black achievement which can be related to academic success such as lawyers, doctors, artists and entrepreneurs. On the other hand, anti-racist teachers are very critical of this bourgeois view. They argue that anti-racist education must be against the formation of a black bourgeoisie, and believe that teachers should not be involved in encouraging the values of a ruthless 'enterprise culture' (competitive individualism) which belong to western capitalist societies and are no part of black culture. Through social mobility a tiny minority may do well but because of the existence of class structure only a few can 'make it', never the class. Black socialists, then, privilege class struggle. One of their main aims is to counteract the negative images of deviance and criminality which the mass media have associated with black youth, and to promote a more positive image focusing on their vanguard position in the struggle for justice.

In this chapter I have argued that multicultural education stresses knowledge of other cultures, but the point is that people can be well informed and still be racist. It is quite common to have multicultural education without a focus on anti-racism; anti-racist education, however, *includes* multicultural education (what I earlier called 'the interpersonal level') and goes beyond it.

Many supporters of multicultural education that I have spoken to tend to be rather defensive. They object to anti-racist education because they think of it as something 'negative'. It does not give a balanced view, it is illiberal — a form of indoctrination. They feel frightened that a militant anti-racist stance may provoke a counter-productive reaction. Fundamentally, multicultural teachers do not want to see education as a political issue. (They do not realize that their own conservative, apolitical view is actually deeply political.) And from the media they learn that anti-racist education fosters political strife.

But these are weak and flimsy arguments, and the critique of multiculturalism by black teachers and researchers is leading to an increasing understanding of the anti-racist perspective. This statement must be qualified, however. Increasingly, anti-racism is being portrayed as bizarre, extremist, inflammatory, politically divisive. In this morning's paper I read that an anti-racist scheme in one local education authority was being condemned as 'a bureaucratic sledgehammer taken to crack a very small nut... There are a few incidents, but nothing more than what happens anywhere else.'

There is then, only a partial advance. And there are still many questions in this area which are hard to answer. The first question that arises is this: why are the views and concerns of black people so often ignored in the school curriculum?

Chapter 4

Racism and art

The 'grand narrative' of western art

To illustrate the ethnocentrism of the curriculum, this chapter focuses specifically on the teaching of art in schools. Some general remarks about art in Western societies are necessary to set the scene.

In the West most of us are taught a certain story about the development of art: art begins with the Greeks, moves through Giotto and the Renaissance, to 'modern art'. There is an implicit notion of 'progress' in this view of art history which has been influenced, perhaps, by similar beliefs about science.

In this 'grand narrative' the arts of what are called the 'Third World' countries have only a subordinate place. Art from Africa and Asia is usually seen as static, unchanging, 'traditional' and is usually kept in dull, dark, anthropological departments rather than prestigious art galleries. The dominant culture, it seems to me, sets up a 'binary opposition'; western art is associated with 'civilization'; non-western art is associated with the primitive. In a nearby reference book I look up Picasso. It says that 'his work was strongly influenced by African sculpture with its barbaric vitality'.[1] It is well known that when Western art is exhausted the art of black peoples has been used to revitalise it. Many European artists have drawn inspiration from African sculpture — why is it then that black art has so little status?

On a recent visit to Paris I joined the hordes of people queuing to enter the Louvre, the prestigious museum in the centre of the city which contains the glories of Western art: the Venus de Milo, the Mona Lisa and many other key works. Wishing to see some African art, I went next day to the *Musee des Arts Africains et Oceaniens*. It is worth trailing all the way out to this fairly remote part of Paris to find an almost unknown treasure. I saw very few visitors here apart from a few school parties that were looking at the objects in the aquarium. (Would the *Louvre*, I wondered, allow such a mixing of categories?) Why has this museum been relegated to the periphery?

Now, it could be argued that there is a museum of non-European art in the centre of Paris; the *Musee Guimet* contains the Asiatic art collection of the *Louvre*. Chinese, Japanese and Indian art are accepted as being 'refined'; they are shown as completely separate from European art and no reference is made to African art. There is, in other words, a hierarchy amongst cultures which is expressed in their art-objects. It seems to me that we are socialized into not only an ethnocentric view of culture but a hierarchical view of societies.

Racism in art

European art historians usually present the work of Michelangelo, Leonardo, Rembrandt, Picasso and others as great examples of western art, whilst the art of other cultures is either ignored or categorized as 'primitive'. And yet, ironically, many western artists have been influenced by the arts of Asia and Africa. One can see the influence of Indian and Chinese art on Matisse, of African sculpture on Picasso and Modigliani, of Japanese art on Degas, Monet, Toulouse-Lautrec. I could make a long and extensive list. On the one hand, there is bias, prejudice and discrimination against non-European art and yet, on the other hand, there is considerable 'borrowing' from these cultures — but without acknowledgement. I contend that this is racist.[2]

I want to argue that one of the ways white domination is maintained is through the discourse of Art History. Consider, briefly, two classics of art history, both basic course books in the study of the subject: Ernst Gombrich's *The Story of Art* and Kenneth Clark's *Civilisation*. The first point about Gombrich's book is that its claim to be the history of all art is false. The book contains only one chapter on cultures outside of Europe and that is entitled 'Strange Beginnings — prehistoric and primitive peoples'! One of Gombrich's presuppositions is the difference in value between *civilised* and *primitive*, European and non-European. European art is equated with civilisation; the arts of India, Africa, Mexico are relegated to the level of the 'primitive'.

This view also pervades Kenneth Clark's book *Civilisation*.[3] The title is puzzling: it concerns itself only with the major developments in Western Europe, so why isn't it called 'Western Civilisation'? Both of these books express the belief that the main difference between European cultures and those outside of Europe is one of civilisation versus primitivism. When Clark uses the term civilisation he is referring to an 'advanced stage of development'; and so-called 'primitive' societies are 'uncivilised, cruel, inhuman, coarse' (*Oxford English Dictionary*). My argument is simple: for a long time pre-Columbian, North American, Indian, Chinese, African and Oceanic art has been categorized in Europe as 'primitive' and seen as such. Isn't it time that this view changed?

Let me be outrageous. I would like to 'problematize' the concept of 'civilisation' by asking the question: Is Europe civilised? George Steiner has reminded us that a civilisation that had produced some of the world's greatest art, literature, music, philosophy and science had also foisted on us one of the greatest catastrophes the world has ever known.[4] The Second World War was probably the greatest debacle of western civilisation. The country that gave us Bach, Goethe, and Kant also gave us Buchenwald, Dachau and Treblinka. Steiner underlines the point that the guards at Auschwitz spent their leisure time reading Goethe or Rilke, or playing Bach and Schubert. He poses a question about how we can continue to believe that anything is to be gained by the practice of the arts. Is there a connection between the refinement of the human spirit and the wanton destruction of human life?

Just because we are dealing with ideas about art we must not forget that racism exists on many levels. I suggested earlier that the best way of understanding racism is to conceptualize it on several levels. Let me now briefly recapitulate the levels of racism and relate these in to the arts. Prejudice and stereotyping by individuals takes place at the interpersonal level. Then there is the institutional level; I regard this as the more serious form of racism because it is not just a psychological matter of a relationship between two individuals but involves influential and powerful institutions. An example that comes to mind is the organization and display of art galleries and museums. The display at the American Museum at Bath begins with a showcase depicting the discovery of North America by Christopher Columbus. Thus the history and achievements of the indigenous people are effaced. Just as in schools there is the 'hidden curriculum', there are in galleries assumptions, beliefs, 'implicit messages'. I find it an irony that the early settlers who went to America to escape persecution gave only two choices to the people they found living there: forced assimilation or extermination. I am simply making the point that museums are not neutral but that their organisation, arrangement and display all emphasize certain messages and exclude others. All museums tell 'stories' which contain biases, prejudices, distortions. These 'stories' become institutionalized and come to be seen as 'common sense'. Moreover, they often make an attempt to conceal or 'smooth over' contradictions in society, which is one of the functions of ideology.[5]

Another example of institutional racism in the arts can be seen in the policy and practice of the National Theatre in London. Very few plays about or by black people are performed there. The directors do not commission plays from black writers, nor do they invite black companies to perform. They use few black actors. Not surprisingly, I never see Afro-Caribbean or Asian people there. Black drama exists and flourishes — but only on the fringe.

Racism also exists at a *state* level. Many racist practices are carried out by the state, but as the 'common-sense' view of the state is that it is a neutral 'umpire' above the struggles of contending groups, the state's discriminatory acts are not seen as racist. It is (falsely) assumed that the state is above such matters. The holocaust, the extermination of European Jewry by the Nazi regime, is an example of *state* racism.

Let us consider, for a moment, the issue of state funded ethnic arts. During the last few years the arts in Britain have become an arena of bitter struggle. The dominant approach is still based on a multiculturalist (rather than an anti-racist) view. Multiculturalism concedes that white people's prejudices are a matter of ignorance about black cultures. At the same time it believes that black people's problems are a matter of not having their cultures upheld. It follows, therefore, that support should be given to the 'ethnic (minority) arts'. In practice this has meant some encouragement of 'traditional', usually exotic, arts of different ethnic groups. In this way multiculturalism avoids the crucial issue of institutional racism. It usually defines racism as an 'interpersonal' problem and occupies its time by speculating whether or not it was intentional. It fails to do anything about the underemployment and under-representation of black people in institutions.

In my view this sort of support for 'ethnic' arts is a form of incorporation. Some critics have called it 'benevolent racism'. Moreover, multiculturalism fails to address such issues as Eurocentric criteria in the arts and the economic, political and social context in which the arts take place. One cannot, in other words, separate the state from capital. I will therefore contextualize my remarks and say something about the nature and role of art in western societies.

Art and its function in society

I have found useful an historical typology that distinguishes between sacral, courtly and bourgeois art[6]. *Sacral art* (for example, the art of the High Middle Ages) served as a cult object. It was integrated with religion and produced collectively, as a craft. *Courtly art* (for example, the art at the court of Louis XIV) served the glory of the prince. It was part of the lived experience of courtly society, just as sacral art was part of the 'life-praxis' of the faithful. Courtly art, however, differed from sacral art in that the artist created as an individual and developed a consciousness of the uniqueness of his individuality. Whereas both sacral and courtly art, in their different ways, are integral to the life-praxis of their recipients, *bourgeois art* forms a sphere which lies outside the praxis of life. In the second half of the nineteenth century all that which is dissociated from the praxis of life becomes the content of works of art. The terminal point is reached in aestheticism, a movement in which art becomes the content of art.

Aestheticism must be seen in connection with the tendency towards the division of labour underway in bourgeois society. Gradually, the artist also turns into a specialist. As the social subsystem art defines itself as a distinct sphere, the positive aspect is aesthetic experience, but the negative aspect is the artist's loss of any social function.

What, then, is the function of art in bourgeois society? I am in agreement with Herbert Marcuse's view that works of art are not received as single entities, but within institutional frameworks and conditions that largely determine the functions of the works. In his seminal essay 'The Affirmative Character of Culture', Marcuse argues that art's function in bourgeois society is a contradictory one; on the one hand it shows 'forgotten truths', it protests against a reality in which these truths have no validity; on the other, such truths are detached from reality.[7] The term 'affirmative', therefore, characterizes the contradictory function of a culture that retains 'remembrance of what could be' but is simultaneously justification of the established form of existence. Through the enjoyment of art the atrophied bourgeois individual can experience the self as personality; but, because art is detached from daily life, this experience remains without tangible effect — it cannot be integrated into that life.

All those needs that cannot be satisfied in everyday life (because the principle of competition pervades all spheres) can find a home in art because art is removed from the praxis of life. Values such as humanity, joy, truth, solidarity, are excluded from life and preserved in art. Art projects the image of a better life and to that extent protests against the bad order that prevails. By realizing the image of a better order in fiction, which is semblance only, art relieves the existing society of the pressure of those forces that make for change. Marcuse demonstrates that bourgeois culture exiles humane values to the realm of the imagination and thus precludes their potential realization. Art thus stabilizes the very social conditions against which it protests.

In bourgeois society the term 'the autonomy of art' is used to describe the detachment of art as a special sphere of human activity from the praxis of life. But somehow this concept blocks recognition of the social determinacy of the process. I think we should remember that this detachment of art from practical contexts is a historical process and that it is socially conditioned.

Most contemporary art is modernist and its defining characteristic is an emphasis on 'form'. It is 'art for art's sake'. I want to argue that ethnic art, like most (white) modernist art, emphasizes form. Though a consideration of form is very important, 'the art for art's sake' approach has severe limitations. More and more black people are realising that the focus on ethnic art, an expression of the multicultural view, is inadequate. Ethnic art is 'traditional', it is out of touch, it remains tied to a memory of a homeland and an irretrievable past. But there are many black artists in Britain who have never lived anywhere else. This brings us to the question of identity.

Identity and commitment

A few weeks ago I went to an art exhibition which contained the work of Afro-Caribbean, Asian, Lebanese, Latvian-Jewish and Welsh artists. The exhibition, entitled 'Dislocations' raised some important questions for me, questions about identity and commitment. What are the various forms of dislocation that black people experience? We know that there is a wide range of response to cultural dislocation; some immigrants gradually assimilate or integrate while others want to retain their cultural identity and resist the pressures of the dominant culture. I consciously think of myself as an exile and believe that this is, after all, the salient experience — the vast displacement of millions of people for economic or political reasons all over the globe — of the twentieth century.[8] With most people a complex process of negotiation takes place; many of my black friends feel that to be accepted they have to deny some aspects of their identity. There is often a demotion of one's early culture because one has been displaced. I know that my childhood experiences were not valorised by me. Indeed, some of our painful experiences are repressed. One common contradiction is that on the one hand, many immigrants are highly motivated and feel that they have to be a 'success' (otherwise, why leave your homeland?) and yet on the other hand, the avenues of success are severely restricted.

The issue of identity and 'the self' is inevitably entwined with that of the role of the artist. Some black painters argue that they want recognition as artists, not as black artists. But others criticise this approach — we could call it individual self-realisation through art — as being reactionary. James Baldwin's later work which focuses on his subjective feelings, is an example of this narrow self-concern. I want to suggest that some artists, perhaps, find their identity, or reconfirm it, through their political commitment. Politically committed artists and writers tell us something not only about themselves — problems of identity are expressed unconsciously anyway — but about the world we live in. They see the role of the artist as being to draw attention to the humiliations suffered by blacks, and to try to raise people's consciousness about their oppression.

Views about identity and commitment are related to the problems of the production of art and its reception. If white nations oppress black people, should black artists refuse to work in white cultural forms? To put it another way, can working within established white norms be seen as complicity with white oppression of the black underclass? One problem is that many black artists were born in Britain and have studied in art schools here; they have no knowledge of other cultural traditions. But, in any case, why should they not use the discourses (or meaning-systems) available to them? It could be argued that cultural forms or styles are neutral and that, if this is so, then they could be used by black artists to resist the dominant culture.

There are, however, some artists who believe that their art should be subversive of white norms; they assert that black artists should reject elite art forms and support popular cultural forms. Similarly, 'commercial' styles should be discarded in favour of authentic ones.

It is clear that there are problems not only about production, the choice of 'discourse', but also of reception. What is the reaction of white people to the work of black artists? The latter have been recognised for their excellence in the field of dancing, singing and playing certain instruments — but what about their contribution to painting? My guess is that most people tend to see black art either as a homogeneous category or as consisting of a limited set of stereotypes.

I believe that a new movement amongst black people is gathering strength. Young black British artists are committed not to some unchanging exotic form 'back home' but to the expression of their living culture in this country at this historical moment. Moreover, they are determined to fight the institutionalized racism of the white cultural bodies. They are opposed to state funded ethnic arts, and their main aim is to foster the Black Arts. In this, *black* defines the colour of the politics and not the colour of the skin. Black, like Red or Green, denotes a political perspective.

Whilst multiculturalism is connected with ethnic arts, anti-racism is linked to the Black Arts movement. Multiculturalism provides niches for black people within a racist system; anti-racism is very different, its aim being to root out racism from the system itself. The anti-racist approach emphasizes breaking down hierarchies and traditional methods of working; one of its main aims is the creation of democratic structures.

Some guidelines for good practice

At a meeting recently some of the lecturers wanted to defer judgement on a weak student's teaching on the grounds that the school in which his practice had taken place was 'untypical'. The school in question, a secondary girls' school in the East End of London, is one where the majority of pupils are of Bangladeshi parentage. After I had initiated a discussion on this case, it emerged that the student was having difficulties with his teaching because of his ethnocentric view of music. It was said that his training at a College of Music had been narrow. I regret that my reactions are often slow; at the time I did not think of asking the name of the College so that I could write to it about its narrow curriculum. Now I would ask questions about the adequacy of the course in ethnomusic and multicultural education which the college claims to provide. I think that my colleagues did not even understand the point I was making: it was wrong to blame the school (and its pupils) for being 'untypical' and not consider the student's ethnocentric teaching which led to his difficulties. Indeed, if anti-racist education is to be taken seriously, such schools should be regarded as typical.

Some positive examples can be found. In my experience, there are a few, but increasing, number of schools where art teachers are trying to examine their own assumptions, looking at stereotypes, discussing examples of bias in the media and the hidden messages of art galleries and museums. Important projects have been set up to develop interdisciplinary curriculum links between art and ('Third World') development studies. One such project, 'Art as Social Action', is trying to find ways of encouraging students to question the dominant ideas about art and art education in this country.[9] It is trying to make art in schools relevant to a multicultural society. The project raises issues about class, gender and race at classroom, community and global levels. Moreover, it contains cross-cultural and international dimensions; and concerns such as ecology, the welfare of developing countries, freedom struggles and the peace movement.

As the project is involved in developing teaching materials which foster these aims, let me give a few examples of the range of work that has been done successfully in primary and secondary schools. In one project a group of children looked at dolls as play and non-play objects. They explored the topic of dolls and gender stereotyping, and how dolls have been used to reinforce cultural traditions and values. In another project a group of pupils looked critically at games. They looked at games that divide people and games that can unify them, and they also discussed the underlying assumptions, such as competition and collaboration. Students talked about games that initiate young people into the narrow roles and the dominant norms of capitalist society, but they also learnt that games could be devised to question and challenge dominant ideologies.

Some children studied patchwork (aspilleras, or textile pictures) to develop an understanding of life in Chile today. Others looked at the development issues in the community and wanted to learn how to make silkscreen posters about the dockland areas in which they lived. I visited one school in which some Bangladeshi pupils had made a superb anti-racist banner for the school. Learning how photography can be used to make statements about a particular theme or topic can also be very productive. In one case a class described a play area near the school and then, in contrast, portrayed how they would like it to be. This approach to art stresses the ability of people to work together to change things for themselves.

A group of children looked at the sources of conflict and issues surrounding the English Civil War. This then led on to looking at civil war in a different, contemporary context, Central America, with a particular emphasis on Guatemala. Human rights and land tenure became an important point of connection between the two studies. In both cases pupils learnt how clothing is an expression of people's lives and concerns. Another group went to a museum to learn about the cultural patterns and artistic traditions of Amazonian Indian life, which are rapidly disappearing through deforestation and state and multi-national corporations' interest in the natural resources of the area. The children used the study to reflect upon their own environmental dependence and patterns of consumption and to ask questions about their own needs and wants. All these projects have helped pupils to realize that art is not produced in a vacuum, divorced from the social, political and economic structures of society. For too long, teachers have thought of art as an individual expression about beauty rather than as collaborative work about the human condition. Perhaps we should begin reconsidering the question: what purpose does art (teaching in schools) serve?

I want to argue that one of the aims of progressive education should be to negate the 'autonomy' of art. I believe that art should not form a sphere which lies outside the praxis of life, but should be integrated with the daily life-experience of everybody. From this point of view the creation of art would not be an outcome of the unique individual genius. Art would be seen rather as a productive process in which everyone, potentially, can take part.

Conclusion

Let me sum up the argument of the book so far. After giving some explanations for working-class failure in schools, I outlined some of the sociological approaches that are used in education. I argued that class analysis has some inadequacies and that the dynamics of race and gender must be considered. 'Race', in my view, is not an empirical social category and has always to be thought of between quote marks. 'Race' is the subject and object of racist discourse and has no meaning outside it. Some of the ways of thinking about the relationship between class and race were outlined and then, in the section on gender, I distinguished between radical and socialist feminist analyses.

I then linked the discussion about class, gender and race to the problem of racism in schools and the educational performance of black pupils. Challenging racism is difficult (partly) because the dynamics of class, gender and race are continually shifting, and producing uneven and contradictory effects.

What, therefore, should teachers do? Should they adopt a multicultural and/or an anti-racist stance? It was argued that anti-racist education is more effective because it includes multicultural education and goes beyond it. To exemplify some of the points in the controversy I focused on art. It was suggested that pupils are socialised into an ethnocentric view of art, culture, history and that the views and concerns of black people are ignored in schools and society. In my view it is crucial that art should be understood in terms of its *function* in society. Not only does the multicultural approach fail to address such issues as Eurocentric criteria in the arts but it also ignores the economic, political and social context in which art activity takes place. In contrast, the anti-racist approach stresses these features.

There are some black marxists who have argued that everything to do with race and race relations is epiphemomenal — a mere symptom of the underlying reality of capitalism. Oliver Cox, for example, argued that black people are encouraged to think in terms of race, a socially defined category, because it benefits the capitalist system.[10] It is necessary to keep workers divided into fractions by introducing and perpetuating antagonisms between them. Race thus prevents workers from perceiving their common exploitation. My argument is that the term 'ethnicity' is used in the same way. For some time now the state has been attempting to fragment black struggle. Its policy is to focus on African, Asian, West Indian and other 'ethnic' groups so as to stress their differences. The Black Arts movement is against this policy; it strives towards that holism which capitalism denies. This new movement stresses the unity of black people; it recognizes that there is a symbiotic relationship between art and the dynamics of race, class and gender. It believes that the eradication of racism involves the creation of a new type of society, one that involves the common ownership of the means of social production, distribution and exchange and the democratic involvement and participation of all hitherto oppressed and exploited groups.[11]

Chapter 5

Ideologies of racism

The concept of ideology

This chapter examines some of the discourses or ideologies that are constantly being used to confuse, mislead, divert, estrange, divide, co-op, oppress black people. I want to look at how the concept of racial prejudice is used in social psychology, and then consider other ideological concepts such as 'equal opportunities' and 'ethnicity'.

First, what do I mean by ideology? It is difficult to write about it briefly because many thinkers have developed differing theories about the concept. Ideology is to do with ideas. Ideas have social roots and perform social functions. Ideologies provide the ideas — 'true' or 'false' — within which men and women think about society and their place in it. We can think of ideologies as the frameworks of thought which are used in society to figure out, explain, make sense of, or give meaning to the social and political world. These frameworks both enable us to make sense of the perplexing events and relationships and, inevitably, impose certain 'ways of looking' on these events and relationships which we are struggling to make sense of. Without these frameworks we could not make sense of the world at all.[1]

Karl Marx insisted that ideas have no independent or autonomous status but are, ultimately, expressions of the material relationships in society. This is the meaning of the famous phrase 'It is not consciousness which determines being but ... being which determines consciousness'. Secondly, Marx identified ideology with classes; above all, with the dominance of one class/set of ideas and the subjection of another class/set of ideas to it.

Marx stressed the fact that the ruling ideas are the ideas of the ruling class. The ruling class dominates because it controls mental production. (This is one of the reasons why the division between mental and manual labour is important.) And we should not forget that the dominated classes often reproduce the ideas of the ruling class.

All ideologies are to do with 'ideas' but not all ideas are ideologies. I believe that Marx's negative or critical conception of ideology is a useful one. Marx laid down two conditions to be satisfied for ideology to be present: the objective concealment of contradictions, and the interest of the dominant class. Ideology is not a simple error. It is a particular kind of distortion, dependent upon real contradictions, which demands their solution in practice before it can be overcome.[2]

The negative concept of ideology is often associated with the notion of 'false consciousness'. One inadequacy of this view is that it assumes that illusory ideas can be put right, or simply replaced by 'true consciousness'. As I said earlier, ideologies hide or conceal contradictions. Mystifications will continue until the material contradictions have been resolved. A contradiction that cannot be solved in real life is often solved in consciousness (religion, for example).

After Marx's death the concept of ideology was transformed; this can be seen in the work of Lenin and Gramsci, who began using the positive conception of ideology. In this view ideology is a belief system of the working class, or a 'world view'. Holding Marx's negative conception of ideology does not mean that Lenin's or Gramsci's positive conceptions of ideology are wrong. I think they are valuable also. In a later chapter I discuss some of the recent controversial developments in the theory of ideology but now let us begin with an examination of the concept of prejudice.

The concept of 'prejudice' in social psychology

In the Scarman Report, *The Brixton Disorders*, commenting on one of the uprisings which took place in the summer of 1981 in several English cities,, Scarman argues that they were due 'to the ill- considered, immature and racially prejudiced actions of some officers in their dealings on the street with young people'.[3] Note that according to this account, racial prejudice manifests itself only occasionally in the behaviour of a few, isolated individual people. Prejudice is presented as an individualized, exceptional phenomenon, basically an irrational response which originates in ignorance. He takes for granted that society as a whole and social institutions (such as the police force and welfare agencies) cannot be irrational, founded on error and ignorance. Scarman gives an explanation of prejudice in terms of individual errors and wants to deny the fact that institutional racism exists. In this sort of 'liberal' approach, society is assumed to be basically unproblematic; by directing attention to *attitudes* and to individuals it avoids questioning anything to do with the differences in power between whites and blacks.

But what was the historical context in which the concept of prejudice was produced? Julian Henriques has described in a thoughtful article how prejudice became a central component of social psychology through a combination of pressing social problems and theoretical developments which occurred in the United States in the 1950s.[4] The two typical social psychological works on racial prejudice of the period are Theodor Adorno, et al., *The Authoritarian Personality*, and Gordon Allport's *The Nature of Prejudice*.[5] The following premises are common to both books: the belief in rationality as an ideal for democratic society and *the emphasis on the individual* as the site of the breakdown of this rationality and therefore as the object of research.

For Adorno, the threat of totalitarianism came from the fascist right; for Allport, in the McCarthyite America of the 1950s, the threat came from the communist left. The work on personality and prejudice was the key element in social psychology's task of achieving a better understanding of individuals so that those who could not see through communist or fascist propaganda unaided could be more adequately protected against the lures of such misinformation. It would thus further the defence of 'democracy'. To put it bluntly, the study of prejudice provided the comparative new science of social psychology with a crucial role in the cold war.

Allport made a distinction between prejudice and stereotyping. Prejudice, 'thinking ill of others without sufficient warrant', is based on the belief that distortion occurs when a person makes a judgment *prematurely*. Stereotyping produces *inaccurate* judgments through a tendency to attribute characteristics supposedly belonging to a group (for example, black people) to every individual who is considered a member of that group. Stereotyping, then, is one explanation of prejudice, and is supplemented by the idea of premature judgment. Allport believes that erroneous generalisation and hostility are natural common capacities of the human mind.

Whilst Adorno realized that prejudice, like neurosis or nationalism, is a product of the total organisation of society and is to be changed only as that society is changed, Allport's view was simpler: *prejudice could be corrected with the provision of accurate information*. American instrumentality demanded both the posing of the problem and the tools for its solution to be sited in the individual so that the given social organisation could be left untouched.

What criticisms can be made of Allport's viewpoint? Firstly, the approach locates prejudice in the perceptual processes. Secondly, there is a shift in the object of study from the prejudiced person onto the stimulus object. And so we see how the social-psychological paradigm reflects, reproduces and legitimizes the common-sense racism which blames the victim. It thus exonerates white racism. Moreover, within this approach one cannot ask any questions about the social and economic causes of difference between blacks and whites in racist societies such as Britain.[6]

I agree with Henriques' conclusion that with the shift of attention from prejudiced individuals to looking at the objects of prejudice, the notion of prejudice in effect suggests that the problem of ignorance lies with black people as the unknown object rather than with the prejudiced individual as the unknowing subject.

It is in this way that social psychology has contributed to the production of blacks as the problem. Social psychology attempts to explain racial prejudice in terms of error. Both prejudice and stereotyping make use of the same related assumptions in understanding error. The first is that individual errors can be contrasted with correct perceptions and judgments of the scientist. The second assumption is that these errors are to do with 'the information processing mechanisms', the result of the faulty workings of the cognitive mechanisms within the individual.

Another criticism that I want to make of social psychology is the way in which it employs the concept of prejudice when it addresses the problem of racism. Social psychology normally defines racism as 'prejudice plus power'. Prejudice is an unfavourable opinion or feeling formed beforehand or without knowledge, thought or reason, often unconsciously and on the grounds of race, colour, nationality, ethnic or national origins. Power is the ability to make things happen or prevent things from happening. Thus racism is having the power to put into effect one's prejudice to the detriment of particular racial groups.

Several criticisms can be made of this view. Firstly, it appears to endorse the idea that racial groups are real in the sense of being fixed and exclusive. Secondly, in this definition power is seen as a possession rather than a relationship. Thirdly, the definition emphasizes prejudice; it denies the importance of institutional, structural and ideological factors which cannot be grasped through the concept of prejudice. Indeed, this is why the simplistic definition of racism as 'prejudice plus power' is so often espoused by the supporters of multicultural education.

To sum up this section: it has been suggested that the dominant perspective within social psychology is psychological individualism. I mean by this term the tendency to give explanations in terms of the individual's thoughts and feelings rather than underlying structures. One characteristic of this ideological discourse is that it constantly emphasizes *prejudice as an attitude* rather than *discrimination as a type of behaviour.*

Let me give an example which illustrates the way racism is treated as if it were an individual, psychological issue. One current practice is called Racial Awareness Training. White, middle-class people go (or are sent) on expensive courses where they are instructed by 'facilitators' who are really counsellor/therapists. People going on these courses become 'purified'. When they take their place on appointment boards, they cannot possibly be guilty of discrimination — after all, they have attended Racial Awareness Training courses.[7] And so, it is implied that racism has nothing to do with capitalism or the racism of the state. I believe, as I said earlier, that the stress on individual attitudes (such as prejudice) leads to an inadequate understanding of institutional and state racism.

On 'equal opportunities'

In a previous book, *Education, State and Crisis,* I argued that capitalism divides employed and unemployed, whites and blacks, men and women. I believe that one ideological strategy used is that of 'Equal Opportunities'. The first point I want to make is that there is a difference between the struggle for equality and what are called 'equal opportunities' programmes. I think that equality of opportunity always remains 'formal'. Class divisions in most societies can be depicted in the form of a triangle with a small hierarchy at its apex and a wide base consisting of the working class. We all know that capital stresses individual mobility ('everyone has the opportunity to do well, to move up'.) This is what has been called individual logic — it is not class logic; if in fact all the working class moved 'upward' the hierarchical structure of society would shatter.

The second point is this: it is said that equality of opportunity, like a marathon race, is 'open to all', everyone is allowed to compete. I would argue, however, that many of the runners are 'undernourished' and cannot do well. Here it may be useful to think about Pierre Bourdieu's argument about 'cultural capital'. He has demonstrated that some families pass on to their children certain forms of culture, cultural codes and knowledge, which act as a hidden subsidy to their children.

There are major contradictions in the practice of 'liberal' individualism. On the one hand it is stated that there are equal opportunities for all, and yet, on the other hand, racist practices continue to be the norm. I could give many examples, but let us consider a paradigm case from the United States. Racial integration in American schools was designed as part of a strategy to reduce inequality. Well, what happened? The whites moved out of the city centres to racially exclusive suburbs. This 'white flight' has resulted in resegregation. Though schools have an integrated enrolment in Britain, many developments within these nominally mixed schools have tended to perpetuate racial disadvantage. These include the streaming of children into different 'ability' groups, the disproportionate classification of black children as pupils with 'special needs', the racism of teachers which often takes the form of differences in expectations, and the higher drop-out rate among black students. There is also harassment of black pupils: 'Incidents range from name-calling and racial insults and abuse, including graffiti, to violence, ranging from slapping, punching, jostling and assault, to maiming and even murder.'[8] Nor should we forget the discrimination against black teachers. They are being systematically denied jobs, refused promotion and confined to teaching certain subjects because of institutional racism.[9]

Equal opportunity is about trying to overcome discrimination based on gender, race and class. But you may have noticed that other categories are continually being added: discrimination based on age (ageism), nationality, religion. In my view the addition of all these categories dilutes the concept of class. Already certain forms of action against sexism and racism have become acceptable, even respectable, but class is constantly marginalized. I want to argue, in short, that equality of opportunity should be used as a strategy to raise consciousness and to begin building up pressure for social change — but we should remember that it is not the objective. The goal is equality.

I said above that the concept of class is diluted in many ways. One of the ways capitalist organisations and institutions, such as the education system and the media, do this is by stressing the Weberian concept of status rather than the Marxist concept of class. (According to Marx social classes are collective historical agents defined by their antagonistic places in the social division of labour, quite independently of individual consciousness.) In the Weberian view there are so many statuses that that concept of class loses its sharp edge. The question of confrontation between classes is avoided; what is emphasized instead is status. And so, in contemporary societies people come to be ranked according to so many subtle graduated statuses that the question of class conflict becomes more difficult to consider.

'Ethnicity'

I believe that, in rather a similar way, some people finding words like 'race' too confrontational, have started to displace it with the 'softer' term 'ethnic group'. Multicultural or multiracial education is now often called 'multi-ethnic' education. I have noticed that some writers draw a sharp distinction between *racial groups*, those marked out as biological categories, and *ethnic groups* which are defined by a much wider range of cultural, linguistic, religious and national characteristics. It is said that 'the justification for this division is that racial groups are based on immutable, physical attributes which are fixed at birth, while ethnic boundaries constitute a more flexible form of group differentiation'.[10]

Ethnicity is a vague term; it is said to apply to a group aware of common origins and interests. An ethnic group consists of people who are united by shared experiences. By emphasizing the features of life they share, they define boundaries inside which they can develop their own particular customs, beliefs, cultures. Ethnicity, then, refers mainly to the linguistic and cultural practices through which a sense of collective identity or 'roots' is produced and transmitted from generation to generation and is changed in the process.

Here, yet again, we have an emphasis on the subjective experience, the stress on cultural rather than on the economic and political 'levels'. I want to argue that the term ethnicity should be problematized. What is ethnicity? How and why is it being used at this particular moment?

It is important at this point to consider briefly the relationship between ethnic groups and the nation state. Since the French revolution, nationalism has spread rapidly throughout the world. The nation-state has become the 'norm' of social organisation. Indeed, it is often argued that freedom can only be realized through the nation. Marxists sometimes talk of the (transcendence or) supercession of nationalism. They often see nationalism as Janus-headed; it is both progressive and reactionary. They believe that in the future the nation, as culture, will continue but that there will (somehow) be a separation of the cultural domain from the political domain.

Some writers think that the above scenario is highly unlikely because, in fact, there has been a change from nationalism to 'cosmopolitanism'. The argument, in short, is that the structures of nation states are limiting for multinational corporations. Transnational units are making national capitalisms out of date. One is beginning to find the same standardized commodities everywhere, the same communication networks; a general global culture is coming into being.

Against this trend, some social scientists argue that there is a tremendous growth in the number of ethnic autonomy groups who want self-government. They want to break away from the national state that, they say, oppresses them.[11] Welsh and Scots, Bretons, Basques, Corsicans, Kurds, Sikhs, Tamils — the list is very long. Here one should note, perhaps, a contradiction within the United Nations' Charter; on the one hand the UN brings national states together; on the other hand it also enshrines the right of ethnic self-determination. It seems to me that in spite of the huge increase in ethnic autonomy groups, the nation state is still very strong. It is clear that many states often encourage ethnic rivalries and antagonisms in other countries for their own advantage.

In European countries there is a particularly close connection between nationalism and racism. Nationalism is a way of excluding blacks, the aliens, the others. *I believe that the more racism there is in a society the more the oppressed groups cling to their cultural identity as a form of defence.* But black groups face many problems. Unfortunately, some ethnic groups develop a narrow mode of thinking based on nostalgic memories of their homeland — which may lead them to be out of touch with contemporary political realities.

A second danger is from the state which often uses 'ethnicity' to divide people. I believe that, like all concepts, it is being used in an ideological contest. Just as there is a struggle to shift the focus of attention from 'capitalism' to 'enterprise culture', from 'class' to 'status', there is a similar attempt to shift attention from 'race' to 'ethnicity'. My argument is that the capitalist state, at the present time, is using the term ethnicity to stress differences between groups, to create divisions between African, Afro-Caribbean and Asian people. Politically aware blacks, however, want to stress similarities amongst themselves, they want to create a unity so that they can act as a political force. Black, in other words, refers not to the colour of the skin but in an affirmative, positive way to the colour of the politics. In short, I can understand and am sympathetic to the attempt by black people to preserve their cultural identity, their difference. They should, however, reject the state's attempt to use 'ethnicity' as a way of creating divisions between black people.

There is also a danger from those who have taken up fashionable post-structuralist ideas uncritically, and want to problematize the concept of identity. Most post-structuralists have a deep suspicion of identity and have presented a critique of it. Julia Kristeva, for example, has argued that we do not have a single identity. The speaking subject is 'a divided subject, even a pluralized subject, that occupies ... permutable, multiple, and mobile places.'[12] The concept of identity, then, is totalizing; all homogenization is wrong. But if we adopt this plural, unstable notion of identity, what consequences does it have for our politics? How are we to conceptualise the human agent?

Though I believe that ethnic minorities under attack should use their cultural identity as a weapon of resistance, I want to make a qualification.

An emphasis on cultural identity is usually associated with experience. If a minority group focuses only on their 'identity' there could be a neglect of the determining role of structures. Such a neglect can be seen in the 'sociology of ethnic relations', a subject which has had a rapid growth in some universities during the last few years. The criticism that I want to make of this approach is that it presents the relationship between 'ethnic minorities' and the majority population in exclusively cultural terms. Ethnic relations sociology ignores power relations. Its emphasis on culture is divorced from any historical and material context, and from the development of capitalist relations of production. Moreover, this sort of sociology ignores the tradition of resistance to colonialism. I would argue that we must try and develop an understanding of the dialectical relationship between the experience of people and the structures that determine them.

Having introduced the concept of ideology and given an account of how 'prejudice', 'equal opportunities' and 'ethnicity' are being used in political struggle, I move on to a consideration of imperialism.

Chapter 6

Racism and imperialism

I believe that to understand fully the structures of racism we have to study imperialism. What are its psychological effects? What are its historical consequences? In this chapter I want to focus on two key texts. The first is Frantz Fanon's *Black Skin, White Masks*, in which he uses psychological theory and psychoanalysis to explain the feelings of dependency and inadequacy that black people experience in a white world. Though the book was first published in 1952 it is now being reinterpreted as a poststructuralist work and repopularized. The second is Edward Said's *Orientalism* which explicitly draws on poststructuralism, namely the conceptual framework of Michel Foucault. Whilst Fanon focuses on the cultural aspects of the black person and draws on psychology to make his analysis, Said focuses on Orientalism and uses literary studies and history. Both are concerned in their different ways with ethnocentricity and racism, with imperialism and cultural domination.

The Black/White division

Cultural alienation

Frantz Fanon's work was influenced by three modes of thought: Hegelian Marxism, the phenomenology of Sartre, and psychoanalysis. In *Black Skin, White Masks* Fanon describes colonial cultural alienation in the psychoanalytic language of demand and desire.[1] The main theme of the book is about how white people consider themselves superior to black people, and how black people want to prove to white people that they are of equal value.

As there are many topics in Fanon's book, I will be selective and focus on his exploration of four relationships: between language and inferiority, race and class, the child and the family, the Master and the Slave.

Fanon stresses the importance of language because he believes that to speak assumes a culture. The colonized are judged in proportion to their adoption of the mother country's cultural standards. In other words, the Negro (Fanon's word) is appraised in terms of the extent of his or her assimilation. Fanon argues that an inferiority complex has been created in every colonized people.

Fanon begins by criticizing a biography written by a black woman, a woman who tries to bleach her body and her mind. He remarks that it is in fact customary in Martinique to dream of a form of salvation that consists of magically turning white. He observes that every woman in the Antilles in a casual flirtation or in a serious affair, is determined to select the least black of men. What they must have is whiteness at any price. Whilst the negress wants to turn white, the mulatto wants not only to turn white but also to avoid slipping back. The negro, having been made inferior, proceeds from humiliating insecurity through strongly voiced self-accusation to despair.

Fanon then looks at another text, an autobiography of a black orphan, Jean Veneuse, who has lived in Europe for many years. The problem is that he does not understand blacks and the whites do not understand him. 'The white race would not accept me as one of its own, and the black virtually repudiated me. That is precisely my position.'[2] This lack of esteem of self as an object of love has grave consequences. It keeps the individual in a state of profound inner insecurity; before he forms an objective relation, he (Veneuse) exacts repeated proofs from his partner. The essence of his attitude is 'not to love in order to avoid being abandoned.'[3] Fanon comments that Jean Veneuse is not an example of black-white relations, but of a certain mode of behaviour in a neurotic (who by coincidence is black). In my view, these two biographical accounts can be seen as examples of the obligation to confess. The obligation to confess is now relayed through so many different points, is so deeply ingrained in us, that we no longer perceive it as the effect of a power which constrains.

The European has a fixed stereotype of the Negro. It is said that the Negro loves to jabber, and from this view it is not a long road that leads to a new proposition: the Negro is just a child. Psychoanalysts have a fine start, and the term orality is soon heard. A white man addressing a Negro behaves exactly like an adult with a child. Speaking pidgin to a Negro imprisons him, decivilizes him, primitivizes him. Fanon remarks how in the midst of associational tests he inserted the word Negro amongst twenty others. The word brought forth: biology, penis, strong, athletic, potent, boxer, savage, animal, devil, sin. He found that for the majority of white men the Negro represented the sexual instinct. The Negro is the incarnation of a genital potency beyond all moralities and prohibitions.[4]

The Jewish menace, Fanon writes, is replaced by the fear of the sexual potency of the Negro. The Negro has become a symbol of sex. Whilst the Jew is killed or sterilized, the Negro is castrated.[5] To suffer from a phobia of Negroes is to be afraid of the biological. For the Negro is only biological. For the majority of white men the Negro is taken as a terrifying penis. For the European the black man is the symbol of evil. Fanon argues against this view and suggests that the collective unconscious is not genetic but simply the sum of prejudices, myths, the collective attitudes of a given group.

The feeling of inferiority of the colonized is the correlative of the European's feeling of superiority. Fanon has the courage to say it outright: it is the racist who creates his inferior. The Negro enslaved by his inferiority, the white man enslaved by his superiority behave in accordance with a neurotic orientation. Fanon, therefore, considers their alienation in terms of psychoanalytic classifications. In the man of colour there is a constant effort to run away from his own individuality, to annihilate his own presence.

Fanon analysed the dreams of many black people, dreams that express the wish to be white. He believed that as a psychoanalyst he should help his patients to become *conscious* of their unconscious and abandon their attempt at a hallucinatory whitening. The patient should be put in a position to choose action (or passivity) with respect to the real source of the conflict: the structures of society.

Fanon is unusual in that though he undertakes a psychological analysis, he recognizes social and economic realities. He is highly critical of Octave Mannoni, a psychoanalyst who asserted that colonized people have an innate need for dependency.[6] In his book *Prospero and Caliban*, Mannoni reduced all socioeconomic relationships to psychology, and stated that only a psychological approach can properly analyse the colonial situation. He said that because white labourers in South Africa are as racist as the managers, racism cannot be the result of economics, and that European civilization and its best representatives are not responsible for colonial racism. Fanon refutes Mannoni and points out that the displacement of the white proletariat's aggression on to the black proletariat in South Africa is fundamentally a result of the economic structure.

The views of Jean-Paul Sartre often appear in the writings of Fanon. For Sartre the idea of 'race' is entwined with that of class. The first is concrete and particular, the second is universal and abstract. In Sartre's view the subjective, existential, ethnic idea of *négritude* 'passes' as Hegel puts it, into the objective, positive exact idea of *proleteriat*[7].

'The supremacy of the white man is the thesis; the position of négritude as an antithetical value is the moment of negativity. But this negative moment is insufficient by itself and the Negroes who employ it know this very well; they know that it is intended to prepare the synthesis or realization of the human in a society without races. Thus négritude is the root of its own destruction, it is a transition and not a conclusion, a means and not an ultimate end.'[8]

One of Fanon's arguments is that there are close connections between the structure of the family and the structure of the nation. Militarization and the centralization of authority in a country automatically entail a resurgence of the authority of the father. In Europe, and in every country characterized as civilized or civilizing, the family is a miniature of the nation.

For the individual the authority of the state is a reproduction of the authority of the family by which he was shaped in his childhood. Ultimately, the individual assimilates all the authorities that he meets to the authority of the parents. Like all other human conduct, behaviour towards authority is something learned; the family structure is internalized in the superego and projected into political and social behaviour.

Now, a black child in Europe has to choose between his family and European society. The individual who climbs up into society, (white and civilized) tends to reject his family (black and savage) on the plane of imagination. The young Negro subjectively adopts a white man's attitude. When the Negro makes contact with the white world, a certain sensitizing action takes place. If his psychic structure is weak, one observes a collapse of the ego. The black man stops behaving as an actional person. The goal of his behaviour will be the Other (in the guise of the white man), for the Other alone can give him worth. There can be no doubt that the real Other for the white man is and will continue to be the black man. And conversely.[9]

As I have mentioned, though Fanon was very interested in psychoanalysis he was aware also of the importance of cultural factors. He was, for example, conscious of how books, newspapers, school textbooks, advertisements, films all work their way into one's mind and shape one's view of the world and of the group to which one belongs. In the colonized countries the view of the world is white because no black voice exists. Fanon knows only too well the double bind of the people of colour under white oppression: turn white or disappear.

At one point he criticizes Carl Jung's concept of the collective unconscious because Jung locates it in inherited cerebral matter.[10] Fanon argues against a genetic explanation and insists that the collective unconscious is purely and simply the sum of prejudices, myths, collective attitudes of a given group. In short the collective unconscious is cultural, it is acquired, the result of an imposition of culture.

In the collective unconscious of the *homo occidentalis* the colour black symbolizes evil, sin, wretchedness, famine, war, death. It is normal for a black person to be anti-black because, through the collective unconscious, the black person has taken over all the archetypes belonging to the European. The collective guilt is borne by what is conventionally called the scapegoat. White society, associated with the myths of progress, refinement, civilization, enlightenment, liberalism, education, has a scapegoat. It is the Negro.

There are many references in Fanon's work to the Master-Slave dialectic. As Fanon often uses this story to argue that the black person internalizes the values of the white master, it may be helpful if I give a brief precis of this dialectical process. According to Hegel, each self-consciousness aims to be recognized by, and to find itself in, the other.[11] The conflict between them must be a life and death struggle. It is assumed that the fight ends in such a way that both adversaries remain alive. Now if this is to occur, one must suppose that one of the adversaries gives in to the other and submits to him, recognizing him without being recognized by him. That is to say, the Master is recognized by someone whom he does not recognize. The Master, unable to recognize the Other who recognizes him, finds himself in an impasse.

The Master makes the Slave work in order, by the Slave's work, to satisfy his own desires. But to satisfy these desires of the Master, the Slave had to repress his own instincts (for example, the preparation of food that he will not eat), to negate or 'overcome' himself as given. The Slave transcends himself by working or, to put it in a better way, he educates himself. Through his work he transforms things and trans-forms himself at the same time. In becoming master of nature by work, the Slave frees himself from Nature, from his own nature, and from the Master. It is because work is an auto-creative act that it can raise him from slavery to freedom. The future and history hence belong not to the warlike Master, who either dies or preserves himself indefinitely 'in identity to himself', but to the working Slave.

To summarize: according to Hegel it is a fight to the death for the sake of recognition that leads to a relation between a free man and a man who is enslaved to him. Hence from the beginning, man is necessarily either Master or Slave. The difference between Master and Slave exists only at the beginning, and it can be overcome in the course of time. Mastery and slavery, then, are not given or innate characteristics. Man is not born slave or free but creates himself as one or the other through free or voluntary action. The character of the Master-Slave opposition is the motive principle of the historical process. All of history is nothing but the progressive negation of slavery by the Slave. Finally, the thesis of Mastery and the antithesis of Slavery are dialectically 'overcome'.

There seem to be different ways of resolving the Master-Slave dialectic. One way of resolving the problem of oppression presented in the story is to see moral superiority as lying with 'the Slave', with oppressed groups, whose characteristics will provide the basis for the new model and be the source of change. That is to say, the working class, women and blacks will provide the new values, the new culture and society.

Another way is to argue for the moral superiority of the characteristics of the dominant group, the Master. (This is the tactic used by Nietzsche in *Beyond Good and Evil*.) This interpretation rejects the idea of class domination as based on working class culture. It insists that the attempt to base the new culture on the Slave's experience alone is bound to mirror the Master's nature and reproduce the roots of the problem in a new form.

An alternative to the above views is to see the Master's and the Slave's natures as distorted and impoverished and to argue for transcendence of both the Master's and Slave's characteristics. I want to stress that this third model is not one of synthesis (as so many Anglocentric thinkers suppose) but of supersession, *aufebung*, of both the Master's and the Slave's characteristics. In short, we need to transcend the binary oppositions of Master and Slave, white and black, the masculine and the feminine, and try to create a society where there is difference without domination and affinity without identity.

The East/West division

Now let us focus on Edward Said's influential book *Orientalism*. It is important for the following reasons: Firstly, its main theme, imperialism and cultural domination, is rarely discussed in the educational field and I think it ought to be. 'No one', writes Said, 'can escape dealing with, if not the East/West division, then the North/South one, the have/have-not one, the imperialist/anti-imperialist one, the white/coloured one. We cannot get around them all by pretending they do not exist.'[12] Secondly, the book provides an excellent example of the way that some of the concepts of Michel Foucault can be productively used. It illustrates, in particular, the meaning of 'discourse' and 'power-knowledge'.

The Orient is the place of Europe's greatest and richest and oldest colonies, its cultural contestant and one of the deepest and most recurring images of the Other. Moreover, the Orient has helped to define Europe as its contrasting image, idea, experience. The British and the French have a long tradition of what Said calls Orientalism.

What is Orientalism? It is a style of thought based upon an ontological and epistemological distinction made between 'the Orient' and 'the Occident'. Orientalism is a corporate institution for dealing with the Orient — it is a way of dominating, restructuring, and having authority over the Orient. Anyone who teaches, writes about, or researches on the Orient is an Orientalist. Said believes that it is only by examining Orientalism as a discourse that we can understand the systematic discipline by which European culture was able to manage — and even produce — the Orient politically, sociologically, ideologically, scientifically, and imaginatively.

The Orient is not an inert fact of nature. It is not merely there. Geographical and cultural entities are made by historical actors. We should remember, secondly, that the relationship between Occident and Orient is a relationship of power, of domination. It was taken for granted that European culture was superior to all non-European cultures. The trader, the missionary, the soldier was in, or thought about, the Orient because he could be there with very little resistance on the Orient's part.

Orientalism is not just a European fantasy about the Orient, but a created body of theory and practice. Orientalism is a will to understand, in some cases to control, manipulate, even to incorporate what is a manifestly different world. Since the middle of the eighteenth century there had been a growing systematic knowledge in Europe about the Orient. Knowledge of subject races or orientals is what makes their management easy and profitable; knowledge gives power, more power requires more knowledge, and so on in an increasingly profitable dialectic of information and control.

Knowledge of the Orient, because generated out of strength, creates the Orient, the Oriental, and his world. The Oriental is depicted as something one judges (as in a court of law), something one studies and depicts (as in a curriculum), something one illustrates (as in a zoological manual). The point is that in each of these cases the Oriental is *contained* and *represented* by dominating frameworks.[13]

Orientalism, like many of the natural and social sciences, has had 'paradigms' of research, its own learned societies, and journals. Orientalism imposed limits upon thought about the Orient. Even the most imaginative writers of the age were constrained in what they could either experience or say about the Orient. For Orientalism was ultimately a political vision of reality whose structure promoted the difference between the familiar and the strange. On the one hand there are Westerners, and on the other there are Orientals. The former are rational, peaceful, liberal, logical, capable of holding real values. The latter are none of these things. A line is drawn between two continents; 'us' and 'them'. Europe is always thought of as powerful and articulate; Asia is defeated and distant. Orientalism comes to exert a three-way force on the orient, on the Orientalist, and on the Western 'consumer' of orientalism.

To say simply that Orientalism was a rationalization of colonial rule is to ignore the extent to which colonial rule was justified in advance by Orientalism, rather than after the fact. When Napoleon invaded Egypt in 1798 he took a full-scale academy with him and everything said, seen and studied was recorded and published in twenty-three enormous volumes. According to Said, such texts create not only knowledge but also the very reality they appear to describe. In time such knowledge and reality produce a tradition, (or what Michel Foucault calls a discourse) whose material presence or weight, not the originality of a given author, is really responsible for the texts produced out of it. Orientalist discourse includes work by Goethe, Hugo, Lamartine, Chateaubriand, Nerval, Lane, Burton, Scott, Byron, Vigny, Disraeli, George Eliot, Gautier. And then, later, there were Loti, T.E. Lawrence, Forster ...

Amongst the founders of Orientalism were Sacy and Renan. Not only did they create a vocabulary that could be used impersonally, they also established the figure of the Orientalist as central authority for the orient. In time, objective structure and subjective restructure (representation of the Orient by the Orientalist) became interchangeable. The more Europe encroached upon the Orient the more Orientalism gained in public confidence. By the end of World War I Europe had colonized 85 percent of the earth.

Many of the Orientalists believed in the inequality of races and the necessary domination of the many by the few. They often used a comparative framework which came to be synonymous with the apparent inequality of Occident and Orient. The Orient was overvalued for its pantheism, its spirituality, its stability, its longevity, its primitivity and so forth. Yet almost without exception such over-esteem was followed by a counter response: the Orient suddenly appeared lamentably under-humanized, antidemocratic, backward, barbaric.

In his 1853 analyses of British rule in India Marx returns, in article after article, to the idea that England has to fulfil a double mission in India: one destructive, the other regenerating; the annihilation of the Asiatic society, and the laying of the material foundations of Western society in Asia.[14] British imperialism in India was making possible a real social revolution there. Of course, it was sad that Orientals were undergoing much suffering but this was historically necessary if the society was to be transformed.

One of Said's main arguments is that fields of learning are constrained and acted upon by society, by cultural traditions, by worldly circumstance, and by stabilizing influences like schools, libraries, and governments. The Orient that appears in Orientalism is a system of representations, framed by a whole set of forces that brought the Orient into Western learning, Western consciousness and later, Western Empire. It is not surprising that the period of immense advance in the institutions and content of Orientalism coincides exactly with the period of unparalleled European expansion. Orientalism was itself a product of certain political forces and activities.

Orientalism is an influential academic tradition as well as an area of concern defined by travellers, commercial enterprises, governments, readers of novels and accounts of exotic adventure, natural historians and pilgrims. Europeans began to talk about Oriental character, Oriental despotism, Oriental sensuality, and the like. For any European during the nineteenth century Orientalism was a system of truths. It is therefore correct that every European, in what he could say about the Orient, was consequently a racist, an imperialist, and almost totally ethnocentric.

In the nineteenth century, writers on the Orient referred to 'its eccentricity, its backwardness, its silent indifference, its feminine penetrability, its supine malleability'.[15] Theses of Oriental backwardness, degeneracy and inequality with the West became associated with ideas about the biological bases of racial inequality. To these ideas was added Darwinism which seemed to accentuate the 'scientific' validity of the division of races into advanced or backward. Thus the whole question of imperialism as it was debated in the late nineteenth century carried forward the binary typology of advanced and backward (or subject) races, cultures, societies. It was argued, for example, that regions of the earth designated as 'uncivilized' ought to be annexed and occupied by advanced powers.

At first the British and French saw the Orient as a geographical entity over whose destiny they believed themselves to have traditional entitlement. Said describes the growth and increasing power of the geographical societies and their commitment to colonization, and then the long and slow process of appropriation by which Europe, or the European awareness of the Orient, transformed itself from being textual and contemplative into being administrative, economic, and even military. Orientalism accomplished its self-metamorphosis from a scholarly discourse to an imperial institution. Orientalists undertook to advise governments on what the modern Orient was all about. They thus became the special agents of Western power.

Orientals came to be viewed in a framework constructed out of biological determinism and moral-political admonishment. The Oriental was linked to elements in Western society (delinquents, the insane, women, the poor) who were thought also to possess an alien identity. The Orientalist surveys the

Orient from above. Only the Orientalist can interpret the Orient, the Orient being incapable of interpreting itself. Thus the designation of something as Oriental involved an evaluative judgment and, often, an implicit programme of action.

According to Said, the Orientalist provides his own society with representations of the Orient, representations that illustrate his conception of what the Orient can or ought to be, that provide Orientalist discourse with what, at that moment, it seems most in need of, that respond to certain cultural, professional, national, political and economic requirements of the epoch.

The principal dogmas of Orientalism exist in their purest form today in studies of the Arabs and Islam. First, there is the absolute and systematic difference between the West, which is rational, developed, humane, superior, and the Orient which is aberrant, under-developed, inferior. The second dogma is that abstractions about the Orient are always preferable to direct evidence drawn from modern Oriental realities. A third dogma is that the Orient is eternal, uniform, and incapable of defining itself. A fourth dogma is that the Orient is at bottom to be either feared or controlled.

In the period between the World Wars the Orient appeared to constitute a challenge. There were native demands for self-government and independence. Once this happened the attitude of British Orientalists started to change. They began to stress the Orient's use to the Western mind in the struggle to overcome narrowness, oppressive specialisation, and limited perspectives.

At the end of World War II the European tradition of Orientalist scholarship, which had been fostered in the United States, was domesticated. Orientalism began to have a Cold War, area-studies approach. Unable to recognize 'its' Orient in the new 'Third World', Orientalism had to face a challenging and politically armed Orient. And, of course, the national liberation movements in the ex-colonial Orient worked havoc with Orientalist conceptions of passive, fatalistic 'subject races'.

Increasingly, Oriental studies began to be thought of not so much as scholarly activities but as instruments of national policy towards the newly independent, and possibly intractable, nations of the postcolonial world. Modern Orientalists — or area experts, to give them their new name — are now indistinguishable from other 'experts' and advisers in the 'policy sciences'. Orientalism still disregards, denudes the humanity of non-European cultures. The West still considers itself the spectator, the judge and the jury of every facet of Oriental behaviour. Furthermore, Orientalism not only degrades its subject matter but also blinds its practitioners.

To conclude, Said's thesis is not that there is such a thing as a real or true Orient but that 'the Orient' is itself a constituted entity. As a cultural apparatus Orientalism is all aggression, activity, judgment, will-to-truth, and knowledge. It is fundamentally a political doctrine willed over the Orient because the Orient was weaker than the West. Despite its racism Orientalism continues to flourish. 'The fact is that Orientalism has been successfully accommodated to the new imperialism, where its ruling paradigms do not contest, and even confirm, the continuing imperial design to dominate Asia.'[16]

Some remarks on Fanon and Said

I think that one of the main criticisms that can be made against Fanon's book is that he exaggerates the extent to which the Slave internalizes the values of the Master, the Negro subjectively adopts white attitudes. This aspect of his thought (Fanon died in 1961) appears really dated. During the last thirty years there has been an increasing awareness that 'black is beautiful'. There has been a rapid growth of Black power movements and Black resistance struggles throughout the world which have given oppressed peoples a renewed pride and confidence.

Another negative feature of Fanon's book is that he does not place his descriptions of colonial experience in any historical context. The problems of the individual or collective psyche are discussed without us knowing the social and historical facts.

I turn now to the Foreword to the new edition of *Black Skin, White Masks*. Homi Bhabha introduces readers to Fanon from a post-structuralist perspective: 'Fanon speaks most effectively from the uncertain interstices of historical change: from the area of ambivalence between race and sexuality, out of an unresolved contradiction between culture and class, from deep within the struggle of psychic representation and social reality.'[17] I have the impression that Bhabha finds the 'uncertain interstices', the 'areas of ambivalence' and the 'unresolved contradictions' positive features of Fanon's work. Using the language of Lacan, Foucault, and Derrida, the Foreword focuses on the psychoanalytic rather than the political. It is difficult to understand; since it uses the concepts (and expresses the concerns) of post-structuralism.[18] What Bhabha is really interested in is not political struggle but 'colonial *discourse*', how domination and dependence construct the colonial subject, how colonial discourse produces the colonized as a fixed reality which is at once an other and yet entirely visible and knowable.

Bhabha suggests that Fanon simplifies the question of sexuality. Fanon's portrayals of white women often collude with their cultural stereotypes and reduce the 'desire' of sexuality to the desire for sex. In spite of these

73

reservations I want to pay tribute to Fanon. At the time it was written (1952) *Black Skin, White Masks* was a major achievement. I have found useful Fanon's views on the process of self-oppression. Many people who suffer from domestic colonialism within the developed countries express sets of values which turn out to be derived from the exploitative values of whites, or from a simple reversal of those values.

I find Fanon's use of the Master-Slave dialectic a stimulating way of theorizing educational and racial issues. My interpretation, briefly, is this: pupils often express their individual needs by the use of the word 'I'. In order to satisfy this need they are moved to action; they then transform an alien reality (knowledge) into their own reality. It has been suggested that we all want to be 'desired' or rather 'recognized' in our human value. To desire the desire of another is really the desire for recognition. I want to suggest that too often in our daily work we forget the central role of the desire for recognition by pupils and teachers.

Hegel's 'fight between adversaries' refers, metaphorically, to the long struggle between whites and blacks. In the era of imperialism the blacks submit to whites. The whites are recognized by those they do not recognize. The Master makes the Slave work. Blacks transcend themselves by working, they educate themselves. Through work and struggle Blacks free themselves from Nature, from their own nature, and from white domination. Mastery and slavery, then, are not given or innate characteristics. We create ourselves.... All of history is nothing but the progressive negation of Slavery by the 'Blacks'. Finally, both Slavery and Mastery are dialectically 'overcome' by revolution.

It should be remembered that the Master-Slave dialectic is not only a psychological metaphor about individuals but a socio-economic one. Fanon shifts to the latter interpretation in *The Wretched of the Earth* in which he extended his analysis to the need for revolution in the 'Third World'. He says that since the settler defines the colonized person as an absolute evil, the latter can only begin his redefinition of the relationship by similarly defining the settler. It is the coloniser who is in fact responsible for the violence of the colonized. The necessary reaction against the settler's violence generates the collective labour relationship which surpasses that of the atomistic and individualistic colonialist. In the struggle for liberation the colonized comes to transcend the original violence of the colonizer:

> It so happens that for the colonized people ... violence, because it
> constitutes their only work, invests their characters with positive and
> creative qualities. The practice of violence binds them together as a
> whole, since each individual forms a violent link in the great chain, a

part of the great organism of violence which has surged forth in reaction to the violence of the colonizer in the beginning.[19]

Turning now to Said's book: *Orientalism* focuses on the Near East, on Islam, and tends to ignore most of Africa and the Far East — but this is not a criticism as there have to be limits. It seems to me that the book tends to treat British and French imperialism as if they were the same. I would have liked to know more about what distinguished French colonialism from the British form. I have read that the overt superiority of the British colonialist was that of a person who would not in general ever accept on personal terms what he called the 'educated native'. In contrast, the covert superiority of the highly limited French colonial education system created a 'native bourgeoisie' thoroughly identified with French values. These were accepted as 'practically white'. Their poets wrote in French, and their leaders represented the colony in the French Assembly. They thus became completely alienated from their own people.[20]

Said's book is full of ambivalences and contradictions. Orientalism is, on the one hand, a topic of learning, discovery, practice; on the other, it is a site of dreams, images, fantasies, myths, obsessions. My first criticism concerns the status of the Orient. Does the 'Orient' refer to something that was purely a Western construct? Or is there a reality to which the Western construct corresponded only poorly? Is the Orient always the 'Other', alien and incomprehensible? It has been said that Said's Orient is at one and the same time an epistemic formation which it is impossible to get behind or step out of, and the willed product of individual writers.[21] He is determined to present two perspectives, the humanist and the structuralist, at the same time. These problems arise, of course, from Said's use of the Foucaldian framework and of the concept of discourse. It must be conceded that Said is always aware of political and economic power in a way that prevents his theory of Orientalism as a discourse from being idealist.

Secondly, Said's book gives the impression that power and discourse is possessed entirely by the coloniser. This is a very one-sided view of history because there is no reference to the acts of resistance — the many mutinies, revolts, rebellions against the Occidental powers. Significantly, the concepts of class and class struggle are entirely absent from Said's work (as they are in Foucault). For Said, race takes precedence over class and gender.

Both Fanon and Said had childhood experiences which shaped their biographical projects; both are saying that racism is a form of division and domination, and that we must unlearn the dominant forms into which we have been socialized. Furthermore, they believe that it is very important to make *connections* between different disciplines. This chapter concludes with some remarks on education as a form of cultural imperialism.

Education and the 'Third World'

Racial inequalities are perpetuated by the dominance of metropolitan societies over peripheral societies in the cultural, economic and political spheres. Educational systems play an important role in the maintenance of inequalities between nations. Indeed, education can be seen as a form of cultural imperialism.[22]

On the whole it has been the dominant bourgeois version of education (compulsory schooling on regulated sites for a fixed period of time) that has been passed on to the colonised by the European powers. If one studies the literature on education in the countries of the Empire, it is interesting to note that the same rationalisations and metaphors used to deal with the working class are used to justify the treatment of black people.[23] They have inadequate families, 'pathological' norms, uncouth and barbaric customs. And so their traditional skills have to be disregarded, their belief-systems eradicated. They have to be 'civilised', to become 'cultured' according to the definition of the ruling nation.

Many writers in the past have written about imperialism in too general a manner but I think it important to remember the *specificity* of imperialism. British imperialism, for example, has a different character from French imperialism, and Portuguese imperialism is different from both. This means that the cultural norms and practices that have been imposed on the colonised by the imperialist powers differ.

And so the schools of the British Empire taught what it was to be 'British' just as the schools of the French Empire taught what it was to be 'French'. It was largely by means of the 'hidden' curriculum that certain taken-for-granted notions about hierarchies, sex/gender relations, views about life in the city and the countryside were transmitted.

Now, many people may believe that because the Empires have passed away, these processes no longer take place, but this is not the case. Capitalist forms of schooling have continued after independence. There are many continuities with the imperial past in the countries of the 'Third World' today; most of the key features of schooling remain the same. Under colonialism schools were never intended for the whole population, they functioned to give education only to a few. They still function in the same way in most 'Third World' countries. There is a skewing of educational expenditure for the benefit of a few — the children of a small elite who support the party and state. Thus a pyramidal structure is reproduced, a form of stratification that is a legacy of imperialism.[24]

Many accounts of 'Third World' countries give the impression that an impressive expansion in education has taken place. This can be misleading, because the 'increase' is often based on the destruction of existing cultural patterns, and the teaching of a limited set of 'skills' that are useful for capitalism's requirements. When the multi-nationals move on to another country (where there is a more docile workforce willing to accept even lower wages) these 'educational' projects are often dismantled.

Many 'Third World' countries have inherited a Western model of schooling where an academically oriented curriculum contributes to the development of divisions between mental and manual labour. But attempts have been made to integrate academic and practical work in a community related context, for example, Tanzania's 'Education for Self Reliance' and the Cuban 'Schools in the Countryside' campaign. In these schemes there is an emphasis upon encouraging students to go back to the village and use their own initiative and the skills they have learnt to modernise rural life. But one problem is that when work-related educational projects are encouraged they are interpreted as being of inferior status to Western curricula. One of the difficulties, for example, that Tanzania has had in the implementation of its education for self-reliance programme is the inheritance of a colonial legacy, which associates agricultural and manual work with Africans and higher-status white collar work with Europeans.

In short, we can see that whilst schools in the 'Third World' are usually seen as agents of modernisation, they are actually reproducing hierarchies such as the division between mental and manual labour, male and female labour. I think it is insufficiently realised that schooling is *not* a neutral instrument. The dominant bourgeois model cannot be used without corrupting the socialist project.

In a sense this is what has already happened in the Soviet Union, China, Cuba. These countries, at present, do not provide us with adequate models because their educational systems have certain limitations: for example the social division of labour and gender continue, curriculum issues are not fully discussed and relations between teachers and pupils remain hierarchical.

Let me summarise the main points of my argument. Too often in the past education has been Eurocentric. It has taken us a long time to realise that we can't 'read off' from one body of knowledge and apply it unproblematically to another part of the world. It is vital that schools be seen in the context of the social formation of which they are a part. I believe that schools at present are largely a mechanism for the reproduction of social and cultural relations.

Schools teach subjects (geography, history, etc.) but actually produce human subjects. Many developing countries have to prioritise production in order to survive economically. As a consequence educational transformation never takes place; schools often continue to be mechanisms for the reproduction of elitism of class, race and gender hierarchies.

I want to underline the point that an educational system or a culture cannot just be 'taken over' from the old society; it must be transformed. Education will have to be reconceptualised in the context of the culture and the social formation in which it takes place. A new conception of knowledge is required, integrating education and training. We need to develop a wider notion of human capacities. All this means that new subjectivities will have to be constructed. In short, if education is to be for transformation and not mere reproduction, the *forms* of education must be taken seriously. We need to remember that people must use new ideas to change the (mental) outlook of the whole of society. People change at the same time as circumstances change.

Chapter 7

Racism and 'the nation'

Open your Guide books
Come and see the Stately Homes of England
Come to see Harewood House
or Dodington Park.
Magnificent Palaces,
pillars, statues, mouldings,
set out in acres of landscaped grounds.

Lord Harewood, it seems
'appreciates the need to involve the younger generation
and encourage their interest in our national heritage'.
Sir Simon at Dodington Park says
'One isn't well off you know.
One is really only the caretaker for the heritage of England.'

Is One?

One is also the heir of the Codringtons
of Antigua in the Caribbean Sea
who bred slaves, like one breeds cattle
on the island of Barbuda in the Caribbean Sea.

Lord Harewood is heir of Henry Lascelles, a banker,
who lent people money
so they could buy men and women,
African men and women
and bring them to Barbados, Jamaica and Trinidad
to work as slaves on sugar plantations.

Henry Lascelles sold the sugar
that the slaves had grown, tended and cut.
He bought some of the plantations.
He owned slaves himself.

He became very, very, rich.
He built himself his palace, Harewood House.

Open your Guide Books.
Enjoy the 'Heritage of England'
But you will have to imagine the thousands of African people
cutting sugar in the hot sun of Barbados, Jamaica and Trinidad in 1740:
You will have to imagine the slave breeding grounds
and the agony beneath the decks on the slave ships that
ferried the African men and women to the Caribbean.

Imagine them.
Because there is not one single mention of them in the guide books.

The Heritage of England is preserved, conserved and its beginnings hidden.

The Heritage of England
High Tories tell us
Is in danger of 'being swamped by an alien culture'.

But not quite alien enough, it seems
for anyone to remember the blood, sweat and tears
poured into the Caribbean soils
for the Codringtons and Lascelles
To build their fabulous palaces.

Whose birthright are they, my lords?

Michael Rosen; 'Heritage of England'

The 'national past' and colonial rule

It has become quite clear that the nation has become a key term in British
politics and that we are encouraged to understand events — and our relation
to them — in terms of national identity, culture, history and tradition.[1] To a
considerable extent this upsurge of public nationalism reflects the crisis of a
social system which, while its development is leading to the destruction of
traditions and customs, at the same time demands an ever deepening source
of cultural meaning to legitimate itself.[2]

This process is really a structuring of consciousness; it mobilizes hopes, memories, rationalities, fears, prejudices. Among its most fundamental elements is a sense of the past which acts as a ground for a proliferation of definitions of what is normal, appropriate, or possible. In short, there is a social construction of the past and a publicly instituted national identity.

It has been argued by Patrick Wright that, far from being somehow 'behind' the present, the past exists as an accomplished presence in public understanding. In this sense it is written into present social reality as History, National Heritage and Tradition. Wright makes a useful distinction between 'history' and 'the past'. History is an intellectual process, the endeavour to establish the truth of earlier events, whilst the 'past' is a more mythical complex existing in the present as a 'created ideology with a purpose.' In this view the 'national past' is not a free-floating ideology or an illusion. It is an established, material institution reproduced through books, the media, political debates, and schools.

In my experience the main characteristics of mainstream history teaching in schools are: a narrow empiricism, a stress on (great) individuals, an emphasis on consensus and reform, and a taken-for-granted parliamentarism. Though there has been little research into the uses to which history has been put in Britain, it is clear that it provides certain models or 'general sketches' which inform everyday thinking. History in schools has been used to promote a belief in continuity and identity with the national past, reverence for national heroes, and the commemoration of great national events.

It should, perhaps, be underlined that the past is something that is *actually* present; it is present in national traditions, like Remembrance Day, and National Heritage, which includes art and architecture, industrial archaeology, landscape and countryside, artifacts, exhibitable objects, traditions and folkways.[3] The past becomes physically present in the sense that it is 'there' to be venerated as tradition, monument, pageantry, spectacle and display. National Heritage is also associated with preservation, the maintenance of old buildings and the like, but preservation can also be seen as an implicit way of preserving those *social relations* which are taken for granted and legitimated by the 'national past'.

The 'nation', then, forms the primary perspective of the 'national past'. The nation postulates a collective subject — it is the state and place in which 'we' live. But the problem is that whilst this process enables some people to find an identity and a unity, it at the same time produces outgroups. Blacks are outcast, excluded. As one of the slogans of the National Front insists: 'There ain't no black in the Union Jack'.

In a way I'm not surprised about this exclusion of blacks from the nation. Consider, for a moment, how blacks are represented. Black people, according to Philip Cohen, have usually been characterized in one of two ways: either as akin to apes or wild men driven by brutal instincts which had to be subjugated by special disciplinary techniques, or as noble savages or children of nature who were uncorrupted by civilization and should, as far as possible, be preserved in their separate and primitive state. It would be wrong to think that the idealized picture of the noble savage was a more enlightened or less racist view than the derogatory image of the ape. They were two sides of the same coin; in both cases black people were made to lack reason and morality. These remained the sole prerogative of the English as a master race.

What we have here is a racist double standard, applied initially to discriminate between African (ape) and American Indian (noble savage). This distinction was later used as a means of drawing the line between bad and good natives. It provided a rationale for that mixture of repression and paternalism which became the distinguishing mark of British colonial rule.

The black, then, is a contradictory figure: half wild, half civilized, an animal with a human soul. In this way the black image is made to conform to the requirements of the civilizing mission, and its peculiar double-bind. Blacks are simultaneously encouraged to evolve into 'coconuts' (objects which are brown on the outside, white in the inside), in other words good hybrids; whilst also being exploited as a support for popular fantasies about racial miscegenation and monstrous birth rates.[4]

As I mentioned in the last chapter, blacks were encouraged to become 'white' through a period of training in the colonial education system. In India, for example, from about 1835, a thoroughly English educational system was introduced whose purpose was to create, in Macaulay's words 'a class of persons Indian in blood and colour, but English in taste, in opinions, in morals and in intellect.'[5] The Indian official was trained in mind and body, to be as able as any Englishman but, however anglicized, he was always barred from the uppermost posts of the Raj. He was a stranger in his own land.

The late-nineteenth century empires were too large and too far flung to be ruled by a handful of nationals. Moreover, in tandem with capitalism, the state was rapidly multiplying its functions, in both metropoles and the colonies. Combined, these forces generated school systems interested (in part) to produce the required cadres for state and corporate bureaucracies.

Racism and class

No one can deny the profoundly racist character of English imperialism, but one of the most puzzling questions is: from where does racism derive? Some writers, like Tom Nairn, believe that racism (and anti-semitism) derive from nationalism, but this view has been challenged by Benedict Anderson who has made a valuable distinction between nationalism and racism. He believes that nationalism thinks in terms of historical destinies, while racism dreams of eternal contaminations, transmitted from the origins of time through an endless sequence of loathsome copulations. Niggers are, thanks to the invisible tar-brush, for ever niggers ... no matter what passports they carry or what language they speak and read.

Anderson claims that 'the dreams of racism have their origin in ideologies of class rather than in those of nation: above all in claims to divinity among rulers and to 'blue' or 'white' blood and 'breeding' among aristocracies. Racism and anti-semitism manifest themselves, not across national boundaries, but within them. In other words they justify not so much foreign wars as domestic repression and domination.'[6]

Where racism developed outside Europe in the nineteenth century, it was always associated with European domination, for two converging reasons. First and most important was the rise of official nationalism and colonial 'Russification'. It should be remembered that official nationalism was typically a response on the part of threatened dynastic and aristocratic groups — upper classes — to popular vernacular nationalism. Colonial racism was a major element in that conception of 'Empire' which attempted to weld dynastic legitimacy and national community. It did so by generalizing a principle of innate, inherited superiority. English lords were naturally superior to other Englishmen; these other Englishmen were no less superior to the subjected natives. Indeed, Anderson suggests that it is possible that the existence of late colonial empires served to shore up domestic aristocratic bastions, since they appeared to confirm on a global, modern stage antique conceptions of power and privilege. Moreover, the colonial empire, with its rapidly expanding bureaucratic apparatus and its 'Russifying' policies, permitted sizable numbers of bourgeois to play the role of the aristocrat — in the colonies.

The above views of Benedict Anderson on the interconnections between racism and class are shared by Philip Cohen. Like Anderson, Cohen argues that racism has its origin in class and notions of 'breeding'. Cohen does not see Anglo-Saxon racism as something first invented by slave traders or plantation owners to justify their exploitation of black people in the colonies, and then later applied to ethnic minorities in Britain. He suggests that its essential idioms were generated from within certain discourses in British class society, which were applied to the indigenous lower orders, ethnic minority settlers and to populations overseas. In short, racism is not something 'tacked on' to English history, by virtue of its imperialist phase; it is constitutive of what came to be known as the 'British way of life'.

Central to the development of this 'internal racism' was the construction of codes of breeding.[7] There is the aristocratic code, which emerged in the late 17th century, linking notions of social pedigree and ancestral blood to a hierarchy of human sensibilities. Secondly, there is a bourgeois version which linked refinement and reason in a new way — it emphasised hierarchies of individual achievement based on inherited differences of 'intelligence' or 'natural aptitude'. This had an important variant, a model of racial degeneration which focussed on certain peoples and places as breeding grounds of vice and disease. And, finally, there is the reworking of these discourses in and through a distinctively proletarian code.

The great fear of the Victorian bourgeoisie was that the concentration of the dangerous (the labouring and immigrant poor) in dangerous places would lead to promiscuity as well as mob rule. One effect of this was that investigation into the real relations between poverty, overcrowding, ill health, and crime became implicated in quite another discourse centred on purely imaginary relations between dirt, disease and the immigrant presence.

With the code of breeding, disease becomes an explicitly racist metaphor, signifying a lethal process of degeneration attacking the health and well-being of 'society'. Ethnic minorities with political demands come to be identified with a highly contagious virus, which must be isolated if the body politic is to survive. It is interesting to note that the strategies of segregation and screening to which black people have been subjected owe as much to procedures for dealing with epidemics like cholera as they do to routine immigration controls.

'The nation' and the language of patriotism

It has been emphasized that one of the ideologies that is used to exclude black people from British life is that of 'the nation'. But what is 'the nation'? Benedict Anderson has proposed the following definition: it is an imagined political community.[8] It is imagined because the members of even the smallest nation will never know most of their fellow members, yet in the minds of each lives the image of their communion. The nation is imagined as limited because even the largest of them has finite, if elastic, boundaries beyond which lie other nations. Furthermore, it is imagined as a community because, regardless of the actual inequality and exploitation that may prevail in each, the nation is conceived as a deep, horizontal comradeship.

The imagined communities of nations did not simply grow out of and replace religious communities and dynastic realms. Beneath the decline of sacred communities, languages and lineages, a fundamental change took place in modes of apprehending the world. Instead of the mediaeval conception of time (the simultaneity of past and future in an instantaneous present),there developed what Walter Benjamin has called 'homogeneous, empty time', marked by temporal coincidence, and measured by clock and calendar.

Anderson illustrates how many acts are performed at the same clocked, calendrical time, but by actors who may be largely unaware of one another. Through works of literature, Anderson shows the novelty of this imagined world that authors conjure up in their readers' minds. He argues that the novel and the newspaper (both first flowered in Europe in the eighteenth century) provided the technical means for 'representing' the kind of imagined community that is the nation. The idea of a sociological organism moving calendrically through homogeneous, empty time is a precise analogue of the idea of the nation, which also is conceived as a solid community moving steadily down (or up) history.

In the twentieth century it has come to be taken for granted that the distinctively modern consciousness of nationality is 'natural'. But in reality nationalism is a historical construct. Patriotism, too, is a social construct and there have been many important shifts in its meaning and significance. For most people patriotism is something extensively propagated by those in authority and is usually associated with the political right. It may seem strange to us that in the eighteenth century, patriotism was the creed of opposition; indeed it was the distinctive mark of extra-parliamentary radicalism.

When, how and why did patriotism lose its links with radicalism and become identified with the political right? Many historians have argued that in the eighteenth century every opposition to government accused the government of corruption. There was a powerful belief that England was the birthplace of liberty. This radical patriotism was no mere rhetorical flourish — it derived from a sense that Englishmen had rights, rooted both in nature and in history, which were being violated. Patriotism, in short, was associated with liberty.

We are told by historians that in the days of Chartism, the language of patriotism was still being employed in defence of liberty against tyranny and slavery. The Chartists argued that parliament did not speak for the people, and that the Government had usurped rights which were natural and which had been enjoyed by the English in the past. One of the characteristics of radical patriotism was its deep rooted suspicion of the state and, in the first half of the nineteenth century, there were numerous issues, such as the New

Poor Law or factory reform, in which the state could be seen as tyrant and the working class as patriots for their rights and liberties.

After the early 1840s, however, the language of patriotism began to pass out of the mainstream of English radical movements. This was largely because there was much less confrontation between the state and the working class. Radical patriotism fragmented with the rise of jingoism in the late 1870s. From that time the initiative passed to the right. The ruling class sought in patriotism a means of diffusing the consciousness of the working class. Patriotism became a key compound of the imperialist state. As Hugh Cunningham has written:

> In the age of imperialism the English were constantly exhorted to be patriotic, and the measuring rod of patriotism was one erected by the Conservatives in the 1870s; the patriot was above class, loyal to the institutions of the country, and resolute in defence of its honour and interests ... Patriotism was firmly identified with Conservatism, militarism, royalism and racialism.[9]

Considerable work has been done in recent years on contemporary conservativism. Bhiku Parekh for example has analysed the writings of Roger Scruton, Peregrine Worsthorne, Enoch Powell and others.[10] (I will be looking specifically at the meanings of 'Powellism' in the next section.) Parekh found that though there are some differences between them, they all share the following assumptions:

First, Britain has been in a state of decline almost since the end of the Second World War. Second, the decline is at several levels, of which the economic, the moral and the political are the most important. The economic decline is taken to consist in low productivity, the lack of initiative and enterprise, and so on. The moral decline is taken to consist in the loss of such virtues as thrift, hard work, self-discipline. As for the political decline, it is taken to consist in the confusion or loss of national identity, a weakening of the sense of patriotism.

Third, Britain's decline can only be arrested by means of a co-ordinated strategy on each of the three fronts:

> The economic strategy consists, among other things, in strengthening the forces of the market, encouraging vigorous competition, minimising government intervention, reducing public expenditure, and curtailing the services provided by the state. The moral strategy consists in strengthening the family, restoring the structure of authority and nurturing the culture of discipline in all walks of life, encouraging women to stay at home to mind the family, requiring the schools to transmit

Victorian moral values and fighting the moral flabbiness of the permissive society. The political strategy consists in fostering a clear sense of national identity based on the unity of 'stock', a common public culture and a strong spirit of patriotism based on a sense of 'kinship'.[11]

Bhikhu Parekh argues that it is this curious and unstable combination of the market mechanism, moral authoritarianism and the racially based theory of national identity that characterizes 'the New Right'. Enoch Powell, Roger Scruton, Peregrine Worsthorne and others believe that the modern state is inherently fragile and subject to constant internal and external threats to its existence. In order to maintain itself, it must develop a strong sense of unity grounded in a sense of nationality or nationhood. What is important is a shared history, customs, ways of life and, above all, an instinctive feeling of belonging to a common kind. In all these writers the term 'kind' means stock or race. A matter of nationality or patriotism is a matter of loyalty to people of one's own kind. For the New Right only the nation can give content and energy to moral and political life; there is, in short, a personal identification with the nation. Since the nation is taken to define the bounds of loyalties, Powell, Scruton and other conservatives reject the concept of obligation to humankind in general.

It is from within this view of national unity that these conservatives discuss the presence of black people in Britain. They constantly tell us that the West Indians do not wish to be a part of British society nor will the latter ever accept them as such. They say that the Asians are deeply attached to their languages and customs and have a different culture from Britain's. Black communities cannot form part of the British nation because they are not just foreign but 'alien' and 'hostile'. The presence of blacks erodes national unity, and subverts Britain's sense of nationhood. The British feel deeply threatened and fear for their unity and integrity as a nation. Surely they cannot be blamed for feeling this way, for is it not inherent in 'human nature' to wish to live with men and women of one's own kind?[12]

Since the black minorities form an 'alien wedge', the 'New Right' advocate the following strategy. There must be a complete embargo on black immigration and every attempt must be made to prevent the entry of wives, children and relatives of black people. Moreover, measures should be taken concerning the blacks already settled in Britain. These measures range from vigorous cultural assimilation to repatriation.

Let me reiterate the basic assumptions of the 'New Right'. First, a state is held together by a sense of nationality. Second, the sense of nationality is only possible among people of a common stock and sharing a feeling of kinship. Third, the black communities are incapable of developing affection for or loyalty to the British nation. Fourth, the preservation of nationhood is a supreme moral value, and it justifies deeds such as forcible assimilation and repatriation of black people.

Parekh argues effectively gainst these propositions and shows that they are untenable. The modern state does not depend on, and has in fact nothing to do with, a sense of nationality. The USA, for example, is composed of people from many nationalities and yet has a strong sense of unity. Whilst earlier forms of political organisation felt threatened by religious, moral and cultural diversity, the modern state tolerates and welcomes them. So long as the different groups acknowledge the established authority and abide by the laws, they pose no threat to the state.[13]

It does not follow that the sense of nationality is possible only among people of a common stock or kind. It is a common historical experience that once the outsiders settle down in a new country, they begin to develop affection for and loyalty to it. This is a process that can be seen in Australia, Canada and the USA. If we think of British history we can see that the English do not constitute a homogeneous stock but are a product of a long process of racial intermingling. Over the centuries different immigrant groups — the Huguenots, the Irish, the Jews — have settled in Britain and become integrated into British society. Not one of them has remained an 'alien wedge'.

We should not forget that West Indians share with the British their language, religion, and a large part of their history. (Indeed, they came to Britain thinking it to be their mother country, and full of loyalty to it.) As for the Asians, it is true that some of their customs, religions and cultural practices are different but surely these differences do not threaten the integrity of the British state? It is usually admitted that they are industrious, entrepreneurial, and that they possess many petty-bourgeois virtues.

Moreover, it should be remembered that customs and practices are never static. As people settle down in a new environment, they undergo a process of cultural adaptation and come closer to the host communities.

'Host communities' is Parekh's phrase. I disapprove of this term because it implies that black people are 'guests'. Guests must not prolong their visit, they have no right to stay and can be asked to leave. Though I agree, broadly, with Parekh's analysis I reject several of his presuppositions. He takes it for granted, for example, that given time black people will slowly assimilate. But why does he assume that this should be the case? There is no reference in his article to the possibility, the desirability, of cultural pluralism. Moreover, he ignores the sad fact that it is because minority groups feel threatened that they hold on more strongly to their cultural identity and values.

You may have noticed that he refers to West Indians and Asians as separate groups; he stresses their differences rather than their similarities. I believe he should have stressed the latter, thus drawing attention to the need for political unity and to underline the fact that 'the blacks', like 'the reds' or 'the greens', is a political category.

Parekh's article is, I believe, addressed to white liberals. He obviously wants to assure white people about the reasonableness of the black case. He points out that Asians are not a threat; they have, after all, petty-bourgeois values. I think this is a clue to Parekh's own political position. Though he is aware of the oppression of black people he does not want to alter the present economic and social order. Throughout his article he suggests that black people can develop an affection for, and a loyalty to, Britain. But if the minority communities are victims of interpersonal, institutional and state racism then it is hardly surprising that they feel alienated. Finally, Parekh is so keen to put over the idea that 'most blacks go quietly about their business' that he does not mention black resistance and the struggles against exploitation and oppression.

Alien culture and national decline

It is evident that many racists have the capacity to link the discourses of Englishness, Britishness, nationalism, patriotism, militarism, xenophobia and gender difference into a complex system which gives 'race' its contemporary meaning. These themes have been combined by the political Right to provide a definition of 'race' in terms of culture and identity. Basically what has been called the 'new racism' is concerned with mechanisms of inclusion and exclusion — it specifies who may legitimately belong to the national community and those who should be segregated or banished.

The process of national decline is often presented as coinciding with the dilution of once homogeneous national stock by alien strains. Alien cultures come to embody a threat which, in turn, invites the conclusion that national decline and weakness have been precipitated by blacks.

Members of the political Right have often drawn attention to the difference between the merely formal membership of the national community provided by its laws, and the more substantive membership which derives from the historic ties of language, custom and race. As Enoch Powell has said: 'The West Indian does not by being born in England, become an Englishman. In law, he becomes a United Kingdom citizen by birth; in fact he is a West Indian or Asian still.'[14]

It is an irony that the distinction which Powell makes between authentic and inauthentic types of national belonging, appears in an almost identical form in the work of the great socialist intellectual Raymond Williams. In his book *Towards 2000* Williams combines a discussion of race with comments on patriotism and nationalism.[15] For him, as with some members of the Right, race problems begin with immigration — the origins of racial conflicts lie in the hostility between strangers in the city.

As Paul Gilroy has pointed out, Williams draws the same picture of the relationship between race, national identity and citizenship as Powell: 'it is a serious misunderstanding ... to suppose that the problems of social identity are resolved by formal (merely legal) definitions. For unevenly and at times precariously ... an effective awareness of social identity depends on actual and sustained social relationships.'[16] Williams' stress on social identity as a product of 'long experience' prompts one to ask: how long will it take before young blacks are accepted as being black British?

Williams' arguments effectively deny that blacks can share a significant 'social identity' with their white neighbours who, in contrast to more recent arrivals, inhabit what Williams calls 'rooted settlements' articulated by lived and formed identities. Moreover, Williams refuses to examine the concept of racism which has its own historic relationship with ideologies of Englishness, Britishness and national belonging.

The popular power of patriotism was revealed during Britain's war with Argentina over the Malvinas/Falklands in 1982. The right-wing journalist Peregrine Worsthorne wrote: 'Most Britons today identify more easily with those of the same stock 8,000 miles away ... than they do with West Indian or Asian immigrants living next door.'[17] Conservative thinkers are usually quite open about their beliefs on race and national belonging. It is the British Left that has an ambiguous position. Socialists seem trapped between a formal declaration of internationalism and the lure of a pragmatic, popular patriotism. During the Falklands war Eric Hobsbawm, an eminent historian and a guru of the Communist party, wrote in favour of a left patriotism, arguing that it was dangerous to leave patriotism exclusively to the right:

> The dangers of ... patriotism always were and still are obvious, not least because it was and is enormously vulnerable to ruling class jingoism, to anti foreign nationalism and of course in our days to racism ... The reason why nobody pays much attention to the, let's call it, jingoism of the chartists is that it was combined with and masked by an enormous militant class consciousness. It's when the two are separated, that the dangers are particularly obvious. Conversely, when the two go together in harness, they multiply not only the force of the working class but its capacity to place itself at the head of a broad coalition for social change

and they even give it the possibility of wrestling hegemony from the class enemy.[18]

The political danger in this approach is twofold. Its enthusiasm for the language of the nation leads to connections between British nationalism and British racism being overlooked. Contemporary racism is either unseen or felt to be unworthy of detailed discussion. Secondly, when there is pressure on the Left to make a populist appeal to match the authoritarian populist appeal to the Right, there is the risk that forms of nationalism which have racial connotations will be endorsed. Unfortunately, the types of subjectivity which nationalisms bring into being and put to work are accepted uncritically.

The themes of national culture and identity have long histories inside the Conservative political tradition. What 'Powellism' did was to construct the black presence as Other, a problem or threat, against which a homogeneous white, national 'we' could be unified. 'Race' and nation have now become elements in a rhetoric of order through which modern conservatism can voice populist protest against Britain's post-imperial plight. The conception of nationhood which the Right holds involves a distinct theory of culture and identity which has been described as ethnic absolutism. This view assumes that nations are culturally homogeneous. It tends to deny that race is a meaningful biological concept — it sees race as a cultural category.

Education and the cultural view of 'race'

The cultural view of 'race has been expressed in articles by Ray Honeyford, a former Headteacher, whose antipathy towards anti- racism is second only to his patriotic reverence for the sanctity of British culture.[19] He stresses the role of schools for socializing 'Afro-Asian settler children' into British mores. Indeed, for Honeyford, the presence of these alien children is an impediment to the education of white children.

Let me give an example of what I mean by 'the cultural view of race'. In 1987 some white parents boycotted a predominantly Asian school in Dewsbury, Yorkshire, England. The parents denied that their protest was 'racial' and claimed that it was 'cultural'. According to the press, the parents were concerned about language problems, the absence of large numbers of pupils during two weeks of Muslim festivals, and the lack of emphasis on Christian teaching (*The Guardian*, 4th September, 1987, p.1). The parents believed that their youngsters' cultural upbringing would be at risk. One of the protest leaders declared: 'We are talking about education standards — just education standards ... There is no question of racialism.'

The Daily Express, however, took a different view; its front page declared 'Parents battle to keep children out of classes which are 85% Asian. RACE SIT-IN AT SCHOOL. Angry parents forced their children to stage a day-long school sit-in yesterday over race ratios.' (*Daily Express*, 4th September 1987, p.1.) The leader writer in the 'Opinion' column supported the parents' campaign but insisted it was about race:

> 'Most parents will sympathize with those rebelling against the Kirklees Education Authority. The parents, mainly white, who do not wish their children to go to a school where 85 per cent of the pupils are Asian are simply thinking of their educational and cultural well being. And what parents do not care passionately about that? Race has nothing to do with the argument, say the parents. But of course it does. It is silly to pretend otherwise. Mr Ray Honeyford, the former Bradford headmaster, who has had bitter experience in these matters, understands their concern. He says 'the education of children from the majority British culture tends to suffer in schools dominated by children from ethnic minorities.' (*Daily Express*, 4th September, 1987, p.8.)

Clearly, the campaign was about 'race' and the parents were prejudiced. The press did not seem to be aware that, in many areas, Asian children are often second and even third generation British, and that many of them speak English very well. Some white parents still think that a school with a high percentage of Asian children is an undesirable school. Why are they not made aware that the Swann report and others have consistently shown that Asian children perform relatively better than all ethnic groups — including white — in the state education system? Indeed, some research shows that black children are often more highly motivated and committed than whites. It seems to me that if the issue really were about inadequate educational standards at the predominantly Asian school, then it should have been a matter of concern to all. There should, perhaps, have been an enquiry by the Inspectorate, and if it found that the standards were low, additional resources should immediately have been given to the school.

It is sad that the principle of 'parental choice' can turn white against black in such an overt manner. If the parents' campaign is successful Muslims, Hindus, Sikhs and others may demand their own (voluntary aided) schools. After all, if white parents demand the right to have their children educated as they wish, then black parents can, justifiably, demand the same right. This would mean the collapse of comprehensive schooling and of multicultural education. Though I have constantly criticized multicultural education for its liberal assumptions, nevertheless it is preferable to segregated schooling which divides children according to race, class, gender and religion.

One irony of the situation is that the views of the white parents are supported by some Muslim groups because they too want the right to educate their children as they wish. But not all Muslims in this country want segregated Islamic schools; some of them realize that their children will be living in a multicultural society so they want multicultural schools. If the right to have separate schools is granted then the divisions between white and black people will increase even further. It is odd that some white parents in Britain are demanding segregated schools (of various kinds) in Britain not many years after the long, hard and bitter struggle against such schools in the United States, where they were seen as discriminatory and declared illegal.

To reiterate one key point: the distinction between the 'racial' and the 'cultural' is a problematic one. The 'racial' (biological) view is increasingly unfashionable; it is too crude, too blatant. And so 'race' is now increasingly seen as a cultural matter, about 'ways of life'. To say that a disagreement is not about 'race' but about 'culture' is to imply: 'We are not saying you are inferior (even though we may think it). What we are saying is that we all have our different ways of life. You have yours and we have ours. Why should our children have to learn about your way of life? It's only right that our children learn about the British way of life.'

The absolutist view of black and white cultures as fixed, mutually impermeable expressions of racial and national identity is an ubiquitous theme in racial 'common sense'. Many people continue to believe that this country is, and must continue to be, a major world power. These people link patriotism with a desire for imperial greatness. Ironically, many socialists also invoke the national interest. (But what is this interest? How can it be identified? How is it created?) What is worrying is that the languages of nation and patriotism used by Labour and Conservative overlap significantly.

It seems that in contemporary Britain, statements about nation are invariably statements about race. Even socialist intellectuals write enthusiastically of Britishness. The language of the nation offers British socialists a rare opportunity; through it they can begin to say 'we' and 'our' rather than 'I' and 'my'. But there are problems with these plural forms: Who do they include and who do they exclude? Do they reproduce blackness and Englishness as mutually exclusive categories?

At the present time many social thinkers are concerned with questions about agency. To what extent do 'the people' make history? Who are 'the people' anyway, and how can they be politically constructed? 'The people' always have to be considered in relation to 'the Other'. At one time 'the people' was opposed to 'the mob'; later 'the people' was opposed to 'the ruling class'. It seems to me that just as in the past 'the people' did not include women, the current concept of 'the people' as 'the nation' excludes blacks.

As the discourses of nation and people are saturated with racial connotations, it is not surprising that black Britons (who as a disproportionately underprivileged group, ought to be Labour party supporters) remain suspicious and distant from the political institutions of the working-class movement. There are, of course, different approaches to anti-racist politics but it is generally agreed that the (primarily) anti-racist rather than the anti-fascist strategy has been much more successful. Indeed, there is a danger in trying to overcome racism by stressing anti-fascism. This is because anti-fascism has acquired a nationalist resonance which can boomerang against black people.

Conclusion

Let me summarize. In this chapter it has been suggested that the different agencies of public meaning have produced a 'national past' which has excluded the role and the contributions of black people. They have been characterized as lacking in intelligence and reason. This has justified the 'civilizing mission', the attempt to make black people 'white'. There is no doubt that English imperialism was profoundly racist. There followed a brief discussion about the origin of racism and, drawing on Benedict Anderson, the suggestion that racism has its origin in ideologies of class rather than of nation.

Attention was also drawn to the fact that 'nationhood' is an active presence in the thinking of English conservatives and some socialists. The discourses of race and nation are evident everywhere: in the press coverage of political events, deportations, struggles in the so-called 'Third World'. All are important sites on which the meanings of race and nation are being routinely constructed and struggled over.

One of the reasons why the discourse of the nation has become inappropriate for the black movement and the socialist movement in Britain is that the economic and regional differences in the country are so great that we cannot speak of one nation. There are now two nations: north and south. Another recent development is the fact that capital has begun to organize multinational structures and operations which transcend the limits of the nation state. It is difficult to combat the multinationals when workers' organisations are still trapped within 'nationalist' thinking. There is also the uncomfortable fact that a whole tradition of English socialism has rooted itself in national- popular ideology, only to become actively implicated in the promotion of racist and imperialist ideas.

The next chapter continues the exploration of the main themes — nationalism, national culture and identity and their inter-connections with race — begun in this chapter, and links these themes with current controversial developments in education.

Chapter 8

The New Right, race and education

The growing movement against multiculturalism and anti-racist initiatives in education is deeply worrying. This chapter examines the views and suppositions of some 'New Right' academics and educationalists, the Salisbury group, and the current attack on anti-racist education. It is argued that they have been successful in setting the agenda for educational debate in Britain. The language and ideology of the New Right have shaped the views of many people on race and education. Education is being redefined and restructured accordingly. The chapter concludes with a discussion on the national curriculum and the effects it will have on black pupils.

The New Right

After World War II there was a period in the history of English politics which consisted of a liberal 'consensus'. This consensus was on the fundamental principles of British politics: the acceptance of Keynesian economic policy, of Beveridge's 'Welfare State', and the need for 'equal opportunities' in education through comprehensive schools.[1]

The field of education has always been an important one for the Right. From the late 1960s onwards, the British political Right developed a large number of organisations and publishing groups to propagate its ideas. The publications known as the *Black Papers*, for example, were very important because they provided the groundwork for the right wing attack on education.[2] The contributers (Cox, Dyson, Boyson and others) supported the retention of formal teaching styles, traditional discipline, academic streaming within schools, of public and grammar schools, and they argued against comprehensive education. The ideas expressed in the *Black Papers* were eagerly taken up by the news media to create a new national 'common sense' about what was wrong with education and what was needed to put it right.[3] The press headlined that 'standards' were falling, that children couldn't read and write, that left wing teachers were indoctrinating children.

As I mentioned in the last chapter, since the victory of Thatcherism, we have seen a radical shift to the Right: to (free) market economics, the ideological stress on Victorian values and 'the family'. In the field of education the government has acted decisively. There has been a steady reduction of educational spending, institutions such as the Schools Council have been abolished. The government has developed the Assisted Places Scheme, and has started publishing the examination results of schools.[4] There has also been a rapid growth in vocationalism in schools through the intervention of the Manpower Services Commission. We must also consider the strangulation of the Universities where research has been drastically reduced. Moreover, there has been a protracted struggle with teachers over salaries and conditions which has left them bitterly disillusioned and demoralized.

I want to argue that this radical shift to the Right was ideologically prepared. One important pressure group that helped prepare the ground was the Salisbury group of conservative academics and journalists. Their instrument, *The Salisbury Review*, first published in 1982, is one of the most influential right wing journals at the present time.[5] The members of the Salisbury group include George Gale, John Vincent, Colin Welch, Peregrine Worsthorne, Patrick Cosgrove, Roger Scruton, all at one time or other of Peterhouse College, Cambridge. They write in the *Daily Mail*, the *Sun*, the *Daily Express,* the *Daily Telegraph* and *The Times*. The Salisbury Group, formed in 1977, is but one of a number of New Right groupings, pressure groups, and advisory bodies (such as Institute of Economic Affairs, Policy Studies Institute, Freedom Association, Aims of Industry etc.), which have proliferated in Britain in recent years.

This group tries to refute and counter left wing ideas and advocates a particular version of conservatism. Against the post-World War II Toryism of the 'consensus', they privilege the nation over the individual. They want to justify a society based on hierarchy, privilege, order, authority and discipline. Their writings assert clearly that inequalities in society are the result of 'natural' difference and 'natural' hierarchy. Implicit in this discourse is a belief in the superiority of 'British' culture. The cause of inequality is cultural inadequacy. Equality, then, is neither possible nor desirable and egalitarianism, of which socialism, feminism and anti-racism are seen as only so many examples, is inimical to 'civilization'.

The Salisbury Review is, then, an expression of the discourse of neo-conservatism. It attained notoriety following the publication of racist articles by Ray Honeyford, headmaster of the multi-racial Drummond Middle School in Bradford. A successful campaign by the parents forced him to resign. His views, however, received endorsement when he was invited by Prime-Minister Margaret Thatcher to attend a select forum on education at number 10 Downing Street. His was not a lone voice. This incident should be recognised as part of a concerted campaign against anti-racism which articulated the concepts of 'race', 'culture', and 'nation'.

Anti-racism is constantly being attacked in the pages of *The Salisbury Review* by writers such as Jonathan Savery, Roy Kerridge, Ray Honeyford and David Dale. For these conservatives 'the nation' is constituted by homogeneity of 'culture' and the problem of 'race' lies in the fact of cultural difference. 'Alien' cultures necessarily undermine social cohesion. And so anti-racism is represented as regressive and alien; those who oppose it become the victims of primitive sanctions: 'Anti-racist ideology ... has now attained the status of tribal law ... to resist is to invite isolation, persecution, or execution.'[6]

According to these writers, 'national identity' and 'true belonging' are defined in terms of allegiance to conservative cultural values. Soviet Communism, Western Marxism, socialism, the Campaign for Nuclear Disarmament, the United Nations, Islamic Fundamentalism, anti-racism and the Black populations of Britain, though employing multiple strategies, compose a unitary Other actively threatening the Christian West.

The Christian religion and British culture

In the discourse of the Right the term Christianity is increasingly being used to gain the high moral ground. For example, Mrs Thatcher, when Prime Minister, spoke in 1989 on the subject, in a speech which is fascinating because of the skillful way it redefines Christianity by weaving different discourses together. I will focus on ten short paragraphs towards the end of her speech. She states: 'Recently there have been great debates about religious education. I believe politicians must see that religious education has a proper place in the school curriculum.'[7] She speaks exclusively of the Christian religion and completely ignores the other religious faiths practiced in Britain today. She must know about these but why does she take no account of them? She says that 'the Christian religion is a fundamental part of our national heritage'. She then makes a shift from 'our national heritage' to 'nation': 'Indeed we are a nation whose ideals are founded on the Bible. Also, it is quite impossible to understand our history or literature without grasping this fact.' The Prime Minister is insisting that we are a nation but who is this 'we' and who does it exclude? Will the blacks who live in this country and who belong to religions other than Christianity, never be able to understand British history or literature?

Her speech continues:

> There is a strong practical case for ensuring that children at school are given adequate instruction in the part which the Judaic-Christian tradition has played in moulding our laws, manners and institutions.

> How can you make sense of Shakespeare and Sir Walter Scott, or of the constitutional conflicts of the seventeenth century in both Scotland and England, without some such knowledge?

This reference to history and literature is interesting because it is an oblique way of referring to culture. A link has thus been made between national heritage, the nation and culture.

She continues:

> But I go further than this. The truths of the Judaic-Christian tradition are infinitely precious, not only, as I believe, because they are true, but also because they provide the moral impulse which alone can lead to that peace, in the true meaning of the word, for which we all long.

The assertion that the truths of the Judaic-Christian tradition are true raises questions about other traditions. Are not Islam, Sikhism, Hinduism also valid traditions?

> People with other faiths and cultures have always been welcomed in our land, assured of equality under the law, of proper respect and of open friends. There is absolutely nothing incompatible between this and our desire to maintain the essence of our identity. There is no place for racial or religious intolerance in our creed.

How does this affirmation stand comparison with immigration law and practice? Why are families kept divided? And how does she explain the fact that racial harassment — ranging from verbal abuse to physical attack and arson — is growing?[8] Or that the unemployment rate is twice as high for black people as for white, and in some inner-city areas it is far higher? And the criminal justice system is loaded against black people too, with twice as many black as white offenders being sent to prison for comparable offences.

Towards the conclusion of her speech, she remarks:

I always think that the whole debate about the Church and the State never yielded anything comparable in insight to that beautiful hymn 'I vow to thee my country'.

It begins with a triumphant assertion of what might be described as secular patriotism, a noble thing indeed in a country like ours.

This short extract from Mrs Thatcher's speech shows how she moves from Christian religion and national heritage to the nation and culture; in short, there is an articulation of culture, nation and her definition of conservatism — a strategy, as we have seen, similar to the one employed by the Salisbury group.

Mrs Thatcher's speech on Christianity reminds me of an article I read the other day about an incident involving a Christian headteacher and some Muslim pupils. The article was headlined: 'Muslim pupils sent home for praying'. Did you see it? According to *The Times* newspaper report, Mrs Mary Stuart, head of the 950-pupil Golden Hillock secondary modern at Sparkbrook, Birmingham said that she was well aware that Muslims are required to pray five times a day. 'On this occasion these (two) boys decided to pray in the car park during school hours. The car park is out of bounds. They were sent home with notes asking their fathers to come and see me.' She added, 'As a practicing Christian, I believe Islam is misguided. And I would not be a Christian if I did not believe that.'[9]

Mrs Stuart is Head of a school where about half of the pupils are Muslim and the rest are Christians, Sikhs and Hindus. I would like to ask why a person with such views is Head of a school in Britain? To say that a major world religion is 'misguided' when half the school's population believe in it, is insensitive — to say the least. It is a denial of a multicultural approach which maintains that all cultures and religions are worthy of respect. Nevertheless, the New Right 'experts' on education like Ray Honeyford, immediately sprang to the Head's defence.

The attack on anti-racist education

These New Right experts on education — writers like Caroline Cox, Antony Flew, Ray Honeyford, John Marks, Lawrence Norcross, and Roger Scruton — began explicitly to address issues about race and education in the 1980s. Their publications on education are very influential. Antony Flew has described the multiracial educational policies of (the now abolished) Inner London Education Authority and of Berkshire as launching 'a revolution of destruction against traditional, colour blind education'.[10] Ray Honeyford has claimed that the development of multiracial education has confused education with propaganda.[11] Roger Scruton and his co-authors have asserted that indoctrination was not just to be found in peace studies and women's studies but in anti-racist education too. Some of the above writers have argued that the schools, like the streets, had to become bastions of 'law and order' and that priority had to be given to establishing effective teacher control in the classrooms and to fostering disciplined learning, especially in areas of 'high ethnic heterogeneity'.[12] Why do black children underachieve? The answer is simple: 'the roots of black education failure' are to be found in 'West Indian family structure and values', as well as the actions of misguided radical teachers.[13]

Many incidents have occurred in the last few years which have been manipulated by the tabloid press and television to give the impression that the presence of black pupils is an educational/cultural 'problem', and to give anti-racist policies a bad name by portraying them all as negative, dogmatic, 'anti-British'. Let us look briefly at two incidents, at Dewsbury and Manchester, which have been exploited in this way by the media .

The Dewsbury dispute

The New Right propagandists vigorously champion 'British culture'. This is a position which allows them to deny any charge of racism: 'Surely you can see that we are not hostile to black people but are just defending British culture?' This argument was used in Dewsbury where a group of white parents as mentioned in the last chapter, kept their children away from school, rather than send them to a local one, Headfield, where some 80 per cent of the pupils were Asian. Both Headfiled and the predominantly white school that the parents wanted for their children (which was already full) were Church of England schools. A New Right activist stated that the 'parents want a majority culture education and Christian acts of worship ... The parents don't want Headfield School and don't think education there is based on British culture.' In other words, the parents claimed that the dispute was about 'culture and not race' — a strategic claim intended to prevent the charge being made against the white parents that they were racist.

It is interesting how some controversies repeat themselves. The arguments used by the white parents in Dewsbury are similar to those used by parents who complained about the 'swamping' of schools by Black children in the 1960s. Black pupils were seen then as posing problems in terms of their numbers, their 'intelligence', their languages and their cultures. It was argued that the more Black pupils there were in a school the less the chances of their integration and the greater the hostility of White parents who 'feared' that black pupils were lowering standards. (In 1965 the government acceded to racist demands by instituting a quota system for Black pupils.) Since those years — apart from the fact that in the vocabulary of the Right the word culture has displaced race and/or intelligence — not much has changed.

The Manchester murder

A 13-year old boy, Ahmed Ullah, was murdered in the playground at Burnage High School, Manchester, in 1986. After the white boy stabbed Ahmed Ullah, he ran off shouting 'I've killed a Paki ...' The local authority set up an independent inquiry. It seems that despite the 35 per cent ethnic minority pupil population, the school had very few black teachers. I gather that the pupils, on the whole, did not report racial abuse to teachers and that they were unsure of how or whether it was dealt with. There was no system of monitoring violent incidents at the school.

Sadly, the report into the inquiry was not published by the authority because it feared that legal action might be taken against it. In the meantime, the tabloid press, particularly the *Daily Mail*, sensationalized the incident and claimed that it was anti-racist policies that brought about the murder. The inquiry team had to deny allegations that their report blamed Manchester council's anti-racist policies for the pupil's death.[14] The inquiry team which prepared a report, said that the tabloid press had led the media down 'a colour-blind alley' claiming that a team 'with impeccable left wing credentials' had condemned anti- racist policies. The inquiry team denies that their report (published independently in 1990) suggests that all anti-racist policies should be abandoned because those at Burnage were applied 'in a senseless and counter-productive way': 'It is because we consider the task of combating racism to be such a critical part of the function of schooling and education that we condemn doctrinaire anti-racism.'

The positive feature that has come to everyone's attention is that anti-racist policies can work only if the entire school and community are involved in drawing them up and implementing them. Schools have an important role in challenging racial injustice but they can only do so effectively if they involve students, teachers, parents and the community. As Gus John, a member of the inquiry team, has said,

> 'Anti-racist policies, in themselves, are no antidote to racism. To be effective they need to be drawn up by all the people involved in the school community, formulated and implemented with care, rigour and caution. Above all, they need the support of good management. Anti-racist policies can never be a substitute for good management.'[15]

103

In their attack on multicultural education and anti-racist education, the New Right make use of two different arguments. You will remember that one of the main characteristics of *multicultural* education is that it stresses that the cultures of all people are of equal value and should be respected. As the New Right believe in the superior value of British culture compared to other cultures, this cultural relativism is seen as a threat. *Anti-racist* education, you will remember, focuses on the unequal relations of power. This approach is seen as dangerous because it stresses equality, makes a critique of the present social, economic and political hierarchies, and is committed to social change.[16]

The project of the New Right, it has been suggested by Paul Gordon, is to detach the concept of racism from the social arena and to relocate it in the realm of personal morality.[17] Many members of the New Right reduce racism to individual discriminatory behaviour. Racism, then, becomes not a result of social injustice but a defect of personal morality. They can then argue that institutional racism does not exist. Black people have no one to blame but themselves for their position in society.

The national curriculum and the black child

One of the points I want to stress is that the language and the ideology of the New Right have shaped the media coverage of race and education. And, of course, it is through the media that the New Right has been able to popularise their ideas and set the terms of the debate around education in Britain.

Some of the principles of the New Right — that schooling should be *subject-centred* not child-centred, that education should be run as a *consumer service*, that parents are the best guardians of *standards* and that it is stupid not to consider some children more clever than others — have become key features of government thinking. Current government proposals — for example, to allow state schools to opt out of their local education authorities and seek funding from central government; to set up centrally-controlled city technical colleges; to establish a centrally- determined national curriculum backed up by the testing of all pupils at ages 7, 11, 14, 16, and to give more say to parents in the running of schools — all testify to the influence which the New Right educationalists have achieved in government policy-making.

The changes proposed by the Education Reform Act mark the end of the educational 'settlement' of the 1944 Education Act and the most radical, if reactionary, restructuring of the British education system this century. With the Education Act, the hopes and approaches encapsulated in the Plowden, Bullock, Warnock and Swann Reports have been discarded. The Secretary of State for Education made this quite clear when he recently declared that 'the pursuit of egalitarianism is over'. Undoubtedly there is going to be a tripartite system again based on selection. High status subjects will be stressed in the government maintained schools; low status subjects and vocational schooling will be offered in the local education authority schools.

I am apprehensive about many aspects of the Act but am particularly concerned about the National Curriculum and its relation to the black child. It is not surprising that there is nothing about multicultural education in the national curriculum. The Act does not address the needs of a multicultural society.

The following points should be noted about the National Curriculum:

i   The power of local education authorities to determine policy will be weakened. Many authorities may quietly drop their anti-racist education policies.[18]

ii   A worrying aspect of the Act is the prospect of 'white flight' from racially mixed schools, as white parents exercise their new 'parental choice'. The commodification of education will reduce the pupil-parent to an individual consumer in a market. This is troubling because of the emergence of an education system segregated along racial and class lines with the majority of black pupils confined to 'sink' schools in the inner city. It is interesting that the national curriculum only applies to state schools and not to the independent sector.[19] Why is this?

iii   The Education Act will create structures that will make learner-centred education more difficult. The testing, for example, at the ages of 7, 11, 14 and 16 will affect teaching method. In other words, there will be a stress on the 'product' rather than on the 'process' of education. The emphasis will be on basic skills, learning by rote, the testing of factual knowledge, getting the right answer. The acceptance (however reluctant) of cultural difference will be replaced by 'the unity of the same'. Pluralism of values (even if it was only formal) will give way to the imposition of values, and collaborative methods of learning will be given up to make way for competitive ones. Teachers, having already lost their autonomous professional status, will become mere technicians. The goal of education, or rather schooling, will be the realization of not an egalitarian society but an elitist one. The vision of education as something to do with understanding and critical awareness will be lost.

iv   This brings me to my next point. The discussion of sociological and political implications of school knowledge will be restricted. The national curriculum will have no place for anti-racist perspectives, partly because so much emphasis is to be placed on the testing of core subjects at the ages of 7, 11, 14, and 16. The national curriculum will put greater pressure on black children who will have to conform to the norm of 'Englishness' and 'British culture'.

I have argued throughout the book that , in the discourse of the New Right, the term culture is deliberately associated with nationalism and with the exclusion from the nation of those who do not subscribe to its traditions. The Conservative view of 'common-culture' is a restricted nationalist one that excludes black people.

Much of the work of the New Right is based on the assumption that there is something unique about being British which unites the nation. The Tory pressure group, the Monday Club, for example, has argued that multiculturalism is more of a 'danger' to Britian than immigration itself and has stated:

> ... our regional, class and national differences cannot disguise a deep and underlying unity. It has ensured an unreflective but deep agreement on fundamental questions. Black and white children need to learn, and they can, of the nation in which they live and the forces that have shaped it. Britain has a great and inspiring heritage.[20]

The Thatcher government was so successful in identifying itself with the nation that it could label its opponents as 'political' whilst itself selling its policies as non-political, common-sense, representing 'what every parent wants'.

I contend that the national curriculum is a nationalist curriculum; it will lead not only to a market-based self-interested individualism, but also to an imposed 'common culture'. My fear is that the current restructuring of education will lead to the propagation of a closed and narrowly defined nationalism. There is, at the same time, political pressure in the schools to squeeze out these subjects, like social studies and sociology, which threaten the idea of a unitary British culture or pose alternatives to the *status quo*. Others share my fears. Government ministers for education have made clear their views on the cohesive role of the national curriculum:

> In reality, our proposals reflect a deep-seated conviction that a vital aspect of education is to pass on to schoolchildren our common moral, cultural and spiritual heritage. We want all pupils to understand, love and value this. It seems to me that pupils are sometimes taught to be critical before they fully understand what it is that has been handed on to them, and I deplore the all-purpose cynicism which can result from

this....Pupils should be able to absorb our national heritage and be prepared for adult life and citizenship.[21]

I see the national curriculum as a way of increasing our social coherence. There is so much distraction, variety and uncertainty in the modern world that in our country today our children are in danger of losing any sense at all of a common culture and a common heritage. The cohesive role of the national curriculum will provide our society with a greater sense of identity.[22]

At such a time, I want to ask what happens to the ethnic groups who want to retain their moral, cultural, spiritual heritage as their defence against British racism? I have noticed that members of the Right have started using a new strategy: when a black minority group that is discriminated against protests, the group is immediately accused of demanding to be treated differently. If such a group wants to continue its cultural traditions it is accused by the Right of following a policy of 'separatism'.

The Right often speak of 'our desire to maintain the essence of our identity' but they seem to want to deny this right to others. There is no doubt that the creation of a national identity is part of the political process of establishing the nation. It is not generally understood, however, that people may be seen as having many characteristics. Only some of these prevail. The question of which national characteristics prevail depends on the balance of social forces within this process. Those who have the power to create and rule a nation-state have the most influence in defining the 'national character'. The definition may embody abstract ideals ('liberty- equality-fraternity' for example) and it might satisfy a popular desire to 'belong' but it is linked just as much to the economic and political interests of the definers.

How is national identity socially constructed? Here is a brief description of an event some years after World War I:

A fortnight in advance of Empire Day we were asked to teach our classes Rule Britannia ... We were given outline maps of the world and the pupils coloured the British possessions red ... Then came the day. Britannia led the way and was guarded by boys dressed as soldiers... Rule Britannia was sung by the school and the head gave a little speech between each verse: 'We are all proud of our flag because wherever it waves there is justice and freedom. In many countries there were slaves but the coming of the Union Jack meant the abolition of slavery.' Enter William Wilberforce, who was duly saluted.[23]

You will have noticed that the children's work consisted of *activities* (singing, colouring, acting) and that they are being socialized through the arts into certain role models. Though they are given some knowledge (a map of the world) it is really their attitudes that are being formed. National identity is being constructed through the ritual celebration of Empire Day (Rule Britainnia, Britannia, British possessions, our flag, the Union Jack).[24] All these elements are articulated with the concepts of justice and freedom — the focus is not on Britain's participation in the slave trade, but on its *abolition* (when it was no longer profitable).[25]

One of the problems of the New Right is that in order to provide a unifying nationalism, they have to presuppose a 'common culture'. The question of a common culture, however, cannot be taken for granted, it is problematic and a matter for debate. There are sharp conflicts about culture between different classes, nations, regions and ethnic groups. Culture is not something fixed and frozen as the traditionalists would have us believe, but a process of constant *struggle* as cultures interact with each other and are affected by economic, political and social factors.

It is very important for people to realize that the reality construction of a common culture or the national character is not something that is established once and for all. Rather, there is a constant process of asserting, questioning and redefining national identity. We should remember that definitions of what the nation and society are are being repeated daily, hourly — but there are also counter-definitions and alternative conceptions of society.

Conclusion

In this chapter I have looked at some Right wing interventions in education. It has been argued that the present radical shift was ideologically prepared by the Right. The views of one pressure group, the *Salisbury Review*/Group were discussed. These New Right 'experts' have waged a campaign against multicultural and anti-racist education since the early 1980s and have shaped the coverage of race and education in the mass media. The New Right have successfully set the terms of the debate around education in Britain.

To summarize: after World War II there was a consensus about politics and education. There was also an implicit agreement between the political parties on their views about black people, which were racist, and this view was expressed in *state policy*. As many commentators have pointed out, state policy moved from assimilation to its more subtle form, integration. And when that, too, failed there was a move towards 'cultural pluralism'. This situation was expressed by the tacit acceptance (and in a tokenistic way) of multicultural education. Just as there had been an attack on 'the politics of consensus' in education, there is now an attack on anti-racist education. Many events have been used by the media to present anti-racist education as an incorrect, dogmatic activity. I think that these incidents are external manifestations of the deep institutional and structural racism in Britain today and that *state policy is switching back from cultural pluralism to assimilation.* Incidents such as those occurring in Brent, Dewsbury and Manchester have been used to question the validity of anti-racist policies nationally.

This regressive move is expressed, I believe, in the Education Reform Act which is not only anti-educational but also anti-democratic. I agree with the view that the proposed national curriculum

> ... reflects an imperialist and eurocentric concept of a static anglo-saxon culture which no longer exists. No matter how it is put together, it will inevitably ignore the contributions to knowledge (be it in mathematics, science or literature) of Black people that have helped to shape today's society.[26]

We hear so much about the national curriculum these days that I wonder when we are going to start talking about the international curriculum. I believe that there must be a vigorous attempt by black people to win representation on all public bodies and institutions. Secondly, there must be an attempt to struggle with whites against an Act in which the so-called National Curriculum excludes black cultures.

I have tried to show how in the thinking of the New Right and much of the media, the concept of culture is articulated with nationalism, and the exclusion from the nation of those who do not subscribe to its traditions. In this strategy even the Christian religion is being (redefined and) increasingly used. The New Right presuppose that there is an agreed 'common culture' when really there are bitter ideological struggles based on regional, class, and national differences. I stressed the fact that 'national identity' is a social construction, an invention, and that the concept of the nation has become ideological and exclusionary. It fails to embrace black people.

As there are many dangers inherent in a populist nationalism I want to suggest that all teachers make time to discuss issues such as imperialism. Of course, I don't mean that there should be direct, explicit teacher-directed lessons on these topics. These issues often arise from the work that the teachers are already doing. Even the study of a Jane Austin novel can provide the context for raising consciousness.

Let me give an example. In a recent lecture I heard Edward Said say that the issue of Empire was represented in English literature long before the work of Kipling, Conrad, Maugham, Forster and Orwell. He went on to analyse

Mansfield Park (1814) in the context of imperialism.[27] This novel, about dislocations in time and space, is concerned with people who are trying to make themselves into an upwardly mobile class. Fanny Price moves from a small home in Portsmouth to Mansfield Park at a time when there is economic depression in England, political rivalry with France, slavery in the West Indies.[28] The peaceful, insulated life of Mansfield Park is dependent on the exploitation of black people on the sugar plantations of Antigua.

As the history of the nation is always being re-written, I want to suggest that teachers learn black history so that they can contest bourgeois, racist definitions of the 'past' which are dominant in the public field of meaning. Black history needs to be developed in deliberate and critical engagement with the national past. Secondly, we must try and construct a 'national past' which would play a more positive part in a public sense of identity, a history that is neither racist nor reactionary. Our aim must be to reinscribe blacks positively into the dominant 'white history'. Thirdly, we need to draw history further out of the world of books, learning and culture, and draw it closer to the experiential and political arenas of everyday life.

I think that as there are many young people in schools and colleges whose parents or grandparents come from Antigua or Agra, teachers should be more aware of how these youngsters feel when the term 'British people' is used. Do they feel included or excluded? What are the connotations of the words 'Black British'? What is the meaning, for them, of the Union Jack? I have argued for a long time that semiology (the study of sign and symbol systems) should be introduced into schools.[29] Any tabloid could be used to begin an analysis, for example, of the monarchy and its relationship to 'the nation'.[30] Another example: teachers could ask pupils to examine the metaphors used in newspaper reports on black people. Have you noticed that black settlement in Britain is often described in military metaphors of war and conquest? The 'unarmed invasion', 'alien encampments', the 'enemy within' are often the terms used to describe the black presence.[31] I believe that one of the aims of anti-racist teachers is to encourage pupils to question. Why is there a nostalgia for imperialist greatness? Why do some people feel a need for nationalism and flag waving patriotism? Is it not time that these aspects of Britishness were abandoned?

Chapter 9

Ideology and politics

In the years after the second World War, education was associated with equality, social mobility, child-centred teaching. Education now has come to have new meanings, with connotations of a nationalist curriculum, testing, standards, accountability, vocationalism, as we saw in the last chapter. But we need a theoretical explanation of the processes by which the discourse of education has been taken over by the Right. How has the Right's education policy won the consent of so many people? How is it that its racist policies are regarded by so many people as 'common-sense'?

One way of answering these questions is by the study of Gramsci's work, which is centrally concerned with the domain of ideology and the notion of the *struggle over meaning*. In an earlier chapter I gave an outline of the concept of ideology, and argued that racism is reproduced (partly) through the ideologies of imperialism and 'the nation'. In this chapter I want first to introduce some of Gramsci's key ideas on the social role and function of ideologies and how they 'organize' the masses, and his innovative concept of hegemony. I then examine some of the recent developments in the theory of ideology through the work of Althusser, Laclau, and Mouffe, and their implications for politics — and education is political — today.

You might well ask: why should teachers read this? And what is the connection between all this and racism anyway? My contention is that we need to link the struggles in education with wider social and political struggles and it is because of this that we need a greater knowledge of ideology and politics. I believe that teachers need such a theoretical understanding if they are to make their practice effective.

Gramsci and the concept of hegemony

A few points may help to put Antonio Gramsci in his social and historical context. Gramsci was an intellectual from a desperately poor background. In this respect he was unlike many other communist leaders, who are from the middle classes. Secondly, unlike some leaders who were theorists (for example Karl Kautsky), Gramsci was a theorist and a leader of a large communist party. Thirdly, as he was in prison for a long time, from 1926 to the time of his death in 1937, he had considerable time to think and write. Before the Russian Revolution, Gramsci had thought of marxism as an economistic, deterministic mode of thought, but after 1917 he was inspired by Lenin and the Bolsheviks.[1]

Immediately after World War I the communist revolutions in Hungary, Germany, Italy were defeated and Gramsci was haunted by the problem: What do marxists do when the longed-for revolution does not occur? In a sense Gramsci belonged to the proletarian moment, that moment in Turin in the 1920s when the workers in Northern Italy were the vanguard of world revolution. They really believed that the working class could, and would, transform the world. But the insurrection failed, the moment passed, never again to return in that form. Consider the situation in which he was living: in the East the Russian Revolution though victorious, was being isolated, and in the West the capitalist system was going through a severe economic slump, out of which was emerging a new phenomenon: fascism. Having experienced a mass movement, its bitter, tragic defeat, and the rise of fascism, Gramsci had to work out what went wrong. In the new, unexpected situation new concepts, new analyses, were required.

Gramsci was deeply interested in the social, cultural and political aspects of life — he was not an economist. He made politics the central category of his thought; indeed, he saw politics as the centre of human activity. One of Gramsci's most innovative concepts is hegemony.[2] He took the term from Lenin and developed it. It is a term which can help explain why capitalism is so resilient, how it has a great capacity to change and adapt and still remain (for many people) a viable system.

Gramsci argued that the domination of the ruling class is achieved not only by economic and state power — the ability to coerce — but by the willing acceptance of the ruled. A ruling class relies not only on force but also on a willing acceptance of its rule because it appears to have a moral legitimacy, a right to rule. Hegemony is another term for leadership. In other words, domination is achieved not only by coercion but by consent — the latter being achieved through 'civil society'. (Civil society consists of private, voluntary organisations, groupings and associations unconnected with the state.)

Put in another way, for Gramsci hegemony refers to the processes whereby one class comes to exert moral leadership over the rest of society, so that its own ideology comes to be generally regarded as 'common sense'. This is a strategy for winning the active consent of the majority of the population to policies and practices which keep them in their subordinate place, by making alternative ideas unthinkable, while remaining within the framework of representative democracy and without recourse to overt coercion.

Gramsci argued that in the East, in Czarist Russia, the state was strong and the civil society weak and poorly developed while in the West, civil society was strong and well developed. The revolution in the East, when it did occur, did so quickly by what Gramsci called the 'war of movement'. Because of the complex development of civil society in the West, there would have to be a long 'war of position'.[3]

Gramsci has also contributed greatly to our understanding of ideology. He believed that the term 'ideology' must include the commonsense, everyday conceptions of the world: the often fragmentary, episodic, internally contradictory and incomplete chains of thought which ordinary people use in everyday life to figure out and make sense of what is happening in the world. He argued that the centre of attention must be those ideologies which have influenced the thought and action of the great mass of people, which organize thinking about society and help to form mass consciousness.[4]

In short, Gramsci stressed the social role and function of ideologies. He believed that political ideas 'become organic' when they are absorbed into the structure of common sense and common practice. He emphasized the critical role which the organisation of different conceptions of the world play in the construction and maintenance of hegemony. He insisted that ideologies 'have a validity which is 'psychological'; they 'organize' human masses, and create the terrain on which men move, acquire consciousness of their position and struggle, etc.'[4]

Through the development of many concepts, Gramsci has given us a wider notion of 'politics'. He was one of the first thinkers to realize that there has been a proliferation of the sites of power. We live in societies in which it is not possible to say with confidence or certainty where power is situated.

Undoubtedly, Gramsci's ideas have altered our understanding of politics but one problem is that different political groups 'read' Gramsci in different ways. There are many ambiguities in Gramsci's work and these have been exploited by different groups at different times.[5] First of all, Gramsci's own writings were fragmented; they were often incomplete notes. Secondly, when the work was published it was in 'selections'. Thirdly, the impact of the work depended, in part, on the political configuration of the time.

His work can be divided very broadly into two periods, the early and the late. *The early period* is that of the 'Red Gramsci', the insurrectionist, during which he was influenced by Georges Sorel's syndicalist ideas and was very active organizing the unions and the factory councils in Turin. *The late period* is that of his eleven year imprisonment during which he wrote *The Prison Notebooks*.[6] It was during this time that Gramsci was trying to say new things, to give new meanings to concepts such as 'civil society', 'negotiated alliances', 'hegemony'. This was the period when he extended the meaning of the term 'political'.

On the whole, those who stress the later period find it difficult to acknowledge the militant, workerist, insurrectionary aspects view of Gramsci. Those who emphasize the early period are antagonistic to people who use Gramsci's writings to argue for a policy of negotiated alliances with the women's movement, blacks, gays, environmentalists, nuclear disarmers and other such groups, now often referred to as 'the new social forces'.

At conferences I have recently attended, many people have been concerned about whether Gramsci was a Leninist. Did he develop Lenin's ideas or did he break with them? From some of Lenin's polemical writings it may appear that the state is merely an instrument of the capitalist class. Politics seems to be a means towards an end. For Gramsci, however, the state is an arena where struggle takes place and politics is about individual and collective self-development. Politics is not just about elections but about individual self-transformation. A contemporary example is the way the feminist movement has changed our consciousness of the family, domestic labour, and child care.

Ideologies: Althusser and Laclau

In traditional sociology power was conceived as consisting of message-injunctions by A to B, to do this or that. Current Gramscian approaches, however, stress that power is concerned with the shaping of the whole ideological environment. Ideologies make historical conditions (on which all social relations depend) appear as unchangeable, inevitable and natural. They make 'the order of things' appear universal, coterminous with 'reality' itself.

Reality is not a set of facts; it is a social construct, a particular way of looking at the world established by a culture's dominant institutions. For example, the media define reality; they do not merely reproduce it. In other words, reality is *represented*. The practice of representation implies the active work of selecting, of shaping, of structuring.

It is increasingly believed that things and events in the real world do not contain an integral, simple and intrinsic meaning. Meaning is a social production, a practice. Because meaning is not given but produced, different kinds of meaning can be ascribed to the same events. But in order for one meaning to be regularly produced, it has to win a kind of credibility, legitimacy or taken-for-grantedness for itself. This involves marginalizing, down-grading or delegitimating alternative constructions. As Stuart Hall has said, there are certain kinds of explanation which are literally unthinkable or unsayable.[7]

The power to signify is not a neutral force. The significations of events is part of what has to be struggled over, for it is the means by which collective social understandings are created. Ideology, according to this perspective, has become not only a 'material force' but also a site of struggle between competing definitions. Volosinov, a Russian theorist of language and literature, was one of the first to argue that there is 'an intersecting of differently oriented social interests in every ideological sign. Sign becomes an arena of class struggle. This social multi-accentuality of the ideological sign is a very crucial aspect...'[8]

Gramsci had similar ideas. As I said earlier, Gramsci stressed the point that ideologies 'organize' human masses and create the terrain on which men move, acquire consciousness of their position and struggle. If, indeed, ideologies have this capacity, then we have to ask: how does this process actually take place? One of the most useful approaches for understanding this is through the concept of interpellation formulated by Louis Althusser and later developed by Ernesto Laclau.

For the French philosopher, Althusser, ideologies are systems of representations (images, myths, ideas or concepts). They are not consciously held beliefs but are rather *structures* which act functionally on people via a process which escapes them. (Ideologies are profoundly unconscious. Have you noticed how we tend to accept so many things as 'common sense', 'natural', 'obvious'?) These 'structures' work on us as individuals through the concept of interpellation. Interpellation is a sort of ideological recruitment mechanism.

In Althusser's view, then, ideology has the function of 'constituting' concrete individuals as subjects.[9] It acts in such a way that it 'recruits' subjects among the individuals, or transforms them by the mechanism called interpellation. This is a sort of 'hailing'. When hailed you immediately recognize that it is *you* that is being addressed, and in that process of recognition you also submit or subject yourself to the consequences of the positioning.[10]

Suppose somebody speaks of the 'English people' or the 'Indian people' we—if we are English or Indian — tend automatically to recognize our place within that discourse; there is a spontaneous identification with it. It is clear that in an interpellation like the 'English people' or the 'Indian people', we tend to recognize certain elements which are included and certain elements which are marginalized or excluded. All ideologies seem to perform this work of inclusion and exclusion.

This theory has been further developed by Ernesto Laclau, whose basic argument is this: politically potent concepts such as 'people', 'nation', 'patriotism', 'democracy', 'liberty' do not belong irretrievably to any one class. As well as existing structurally as classes, individuals and groups also exist as 'people' — a term which cuts across class, religion and gender. He argues that no particular ideological element has a pregiven class location: that taken in isolation we cannot designate a particular element, whether it be patriotism, familial duty, sacrifice or opposition to the state as essentially the prerogative of one given class or group.[11]

Laclau insists that ideological elements have 'no necessary class connotation' and that this connotation, or association, where it is seen to exist, is only the result of the articulation of those elements in a concrete ideological discourse, the ways in which elements are articulated together into a relative unity. (Of course, we must remember that an ideological unity does not depend on logical consistency.) The links between the elements are not automatically given or naturally assumed; they have to be persuasively constructed through an immense ideological labour. In a process of ideological and symbolic reorganization, selections, combinations and condensations of various 'available' or 'rediscovered' ideological elements are reworked into a grid of interpellations.

It has begun to be realized that meanings which have been coupled (linked together, or articulated) can be un-coupled. The 'struggle in discourse' consists precisely of this process of 'discursive articulation and disarticulation'. There are many historical examples where the conduct of a social struggle depended on the effective dis-articulation of certain key terms such as 'the nation', 'the people', 'civil rights' from their previous couplings, and their extrapolation to new meanings, representing the emergence of new political subjects.

Here are some examples. The same elementary term 'democracy' can be articulated with other elements and condensed into very different ideologies: democracy of the Free West and the German Democratic Republic. What matters is the way in which different social interests or forces conduct an ideological struggle to disarticulate a signifier from one preferred or dominant meaning-system, and rearticulate it within, different chain of connotations.

It is clear that even though there is no necessary belongingness of the term 'freedom' to the bourgeoisie, a certain class articulation of the term has indeed been effectively secured, over long historical periods; that which articulated 'freedom' with the liberty of the individual, with the 'free' market and liberal political values but which disarticulated it from its possible condensations predicated on the 'freedom' of the worker to withdraw his labour or the 'freedom' of the 'freedom-fighter'.

Sometimes, the struggle in language occurs between two different terms: the struggle, for example, to replace the term 'immigrant' with the term 'black'. But often the struggle takes the form of a different accenting of the same term: for example, the term black belonged in the vocabularies of both the oppressed and the oppressors. What was being struggled over was not the 'class belongingness' of the term, but the inflection it could be given. In the discourse of the Black movement, the disparaging connotation 'black = the despised race' was inverted into the opposite: 'black = beautiful'. In this case the struggle was not over the term itself but over its connotative meaning.

Now, if the social struggle in language can be conducted over the same sign, it follows that whole discourses cannot be assigned permanently to any one side in the struggle. Opposing arguments are easy to mount. Changing the terms of an argument is exceedingly difficult. Arguments which seek to change the terms of reference are read as 'straying from the point'. And so part of the struggle is over the way the problem is formulated: the terms of the debate and the 'logic' it entails.

Laclau uses the argument about the rise of German fascism to illustrate his thesis.[12] He refutes the orthodox marxist argument which sees fascism as a more or less homogeneous ideological expression of the most reactionary sectors of the capitalist class. Laclau believes that this conception, in over-emphasising class, is theoretically inadequate because fascism operated not at the level of class struggle but rather in the area of *popular-democratic* struggle. One of the necessary ingredients for the formation of a popular-democratic positionality is the articulation of a sense of tradition or of heritage in which 'the people' can establish itself as part of a historical and cultural continuity. As suggested in the last chapter, 'the heritage' has to be exhumed and/or reinvented.

Laclau makes a distinction between the abstract elements within a particular ideology and the way in which these are combined in a historically specific, concrete ideology. He insists that the ideological elements themselves are relatively meaningless until they are combined with other signs or elements, and that what is crucial is precisely how they are combined. Consider the elements 'England' and 'liberty'. In one discourse (say, Churchill in 1940) the idea of 'the freeborn Englishman' protecting hearth and home suggests a commitment against fascism, defending from Nazi terror those liberties which did exist in England. But on the other hand, that very idea could be mobilized in the 1970s or 1980s in order to protect 'hearth and home' from the perceived threat of blacks moving in next door — the same ideological elements, but inserted in a very different discursive framework and leading to a quite contrary politics.[13]

According to Laclau the goal or project of a political party is to win cultural and moral leadership (hegemony) by speaking to the people and expanding its objectives and constituency so that it achieves a real popular grounding. It must address the people and establish connections with the lived popular culture. The party, then, comes to articulate its own programme as if it were universal, the programme of the people. And in so doing, the party exerts its own cultural authority by constructing the idea of 'the people' in its own image. In short, Laclau is reminding us that social alliances do not simply happen, they are brought into being by the construction and periodic reconstruction of a common political discourse.

The relevance of Gramsci's thought

During the last few years some intellectuals have been heavily influenced by post-structuralist and post-marxist thought. The concept of class, for example, has been problematized by Barry Hindess, Paul Hirst and others.[14] Many people support 'single-issue' campaigns (such as nuclear disarmament) and reject the primacy of class. Classical marxist concepts like ideology, the state, etc., have been heavily criticized by post-structuralists like Michel Foucault and others. In classical marxism, classes are taken for granted; they are treated as 'historical givens'. But now many marxists argue that classes have to be understood as the complex *result* of different forms of social struggle at all the levels of social practice, including the ideological.

These trends have influenced many thinkers, like Ernesto Laclau and Chantal Mouffe, Stuart Hall, Eric Hobsbawm, who are trying to apply Gramsci's innovative concepts to the contemporary political situation. They are all concerned, in their different ways, with the question: to what extent is Gramsci's thought relevant today? Post-marxists argue that Gramscian thought is irrelevant to us as we are living in a completely different historical period. Others say that an understanding of Gramsci's concepts is vital but go on to modify marxism, to make it 'respectable'.

Having given an account of the key ideas of Laclau and Mouffe, I must state some reservations about their book *Hegemony and Socialist Strategy: Towards a Radical Democratic Politics*.[15] The book is an important one in that it gives us an insight into many of the ideas of intellectuals that are moving to the right. The authors, in fact, claim that they are *post-marxists*. Favouring diversity and complexity, they are against all forms of reductionism and 'essentialism' (that is to say, when the apparent complexity of the social whole is reduced in the end to an original common essence). This means that any explanatory project can be disparaged because an 'essence' (class, or the economy) can always be discoverable in it. They reject thinkers who use categories such as the objective laws of capitalism, class or class interest, the forces and relations of production.

Their argument, very briefly, is this: in orthodox marxism there are two explanations for the movement of history. One, the contradictions between the forces of production and the relations of production. (For an example of this type of argument see G.A. Cohen, *Karl Marx's Theory of History — A defence*, London, Oxford University Press, 1979.) Two, the primacy of class struggle. Laclau and Mouffe argue that these two are contradictory. In the former explanation, class struggle is absent, while in the latter, it is prioritized. Whenever there are problems within Marxism, class is used as a 'deus ex machina'. As Marx's theory of class has many inadequacies, Laclau rejects the concept of 'the proletariat'. There is no universal class in the Lukácsian sense. There are 'workers' struggles', but these are limited. Since the French Revolution new social movements have arisen. There is now a plurality of struggles. The task is to bring them together and construct a new hegemony.

Laclau and Mouffe give a caricatured and impoverished account of what Marxism is. It is reduced to a few dogmatic absolutes and is then dismissed for being determinist, economist, 'essentialist'. They assert, for example, that the concept 'relative autonomy' is invalid. In a counter-argument Normal Geras uses the example of a length of chain that can secure him by the ankle to a stout post. He argues that the chain and post are fundamental determinants of his lifestyle but leave him some scope still for independent decision making.[16]

Another criticism of the work of Laclau and Mouffe is that the spheres of politics and ideology have become subordinate and the symbolic has expanded to be all-encompassing. All the world is Discourse; everything is Discourse. But what are the conditions of possibility of discourse? They do not say. A major difficulty in their work is that it is hard to figure out the basis for any particular political direction that should be followed. As Geras has pointed out, their concepts can supply no useful index of what is progressive.

Indeed, their theory could support any kind of politics. Laclau and Mouffe say they support a radical, pluralistic, democratic politics but they provide no reasons why it should be that rather than something else.

Laclau and Mouffe present a simplistic account of modern history. They go so far as to conflate the whole of Marxism with its Stalinist forms. Secondly, their method is such that any principles of explanation can be criticized and dismissed as 'essentialism'. They believe that a break with 'orthodox essentialism' must entail the critique of every type of fixity. Thirdly, their theory is representative of a new idealism. Everything is Discourse and Discourse is everywhere. They espouse the virtues of a pluralist democratic politics against an authoritarian marxism and have forgotten that it is axiomatic that socialism must be democratic.[17]

Let us now turn to two other thinkers, Hall and Hobsbawm, who also use Gramscian concepts. Stuart Hall has suggested that we should not think of Gramsci as some sort of key that will open all locked doors. Gramsci was formed in the specificity of his own historical period and his thought cannot be simply transferred to another historical epoch with differing conditions. It would be much more fruitful if we focused on ways in which we could appropriate Gramsci for our own purposes.

Hall has done this in his brilliant analysis of Thatcherism. He argues that Thatcherism emerged in the mid-70's and at first wanted to contest the Keynesian welfare state. Thatcherism wanted to decentre it, and then to dismantle it. But, of course, nothing is dismantled without the introduction of new themes. Thatcherism provided people with the rhetoric of (clear, uncomplicated) Victorian values. It constructed a politics, a new 'common sense' which appealed to people and recruited them to her side.[18]

What we have to learn from Gramsci is that politics is about the social, the moral, the intellectual; there is not one aspect of human experience which escapes politics. Politics is hard work. It requires a continual analysis of existing forces and of complex contradictions. One of its main functions is to enlist people. People are not corrupt or stupid — they have to be persuaded. Of course, people have different identities but identities are constructed. And now, in contemporary society, there is a pluralization of social identities. It is not possible to transform society from one site only. As there are many sites, attempts must be made to connect with people's consciousness on different sites. Gramsci believed in the existence not of one homogeneous class but of a new 'historic bloc'. That is why there are many new centres of antagonism to the capitalist state. The media, the family, health, education have all become important areas of contestation.

Another academic who has made use of Gramscian concepts is the British marxist historian Eric Hobsbawm. His position is very controversial. He argues against orthodox marxism and propagates the idea of alliances with various non-socialist groups. He suggests that one way of thinking about hegemony is of seeing it as the high moral ground that has to be won. This implies that the consent of a wide range of groups and classes must first be gained. Following Gramsci, he stresses the point that hegemony must be won *before* the revolution. Hobsbawm gives two contemporary examples. One, the Portuguese revolution of 1974. At the beginning of the revolution power was transferred to the working class, but the capacity for social change was very limited because there was not enough support. The Left remained a minority group. In the Iranian revolution, however, radical social change was possible as soon as the Shah was overthrown because there was widespread, popular support for a fundamentalist Islamic regime.

But what about the political situation in Britain now? In Hobsbawm's view the forward march of labour has been halted.[19] Manual workers are not in the majority anymore. The power of the industrial unions has rapidly declined. He makes the point that the Labour party, even in the past, did not only represent (male) workers. (Indeed, between the Wars, 40% of the party membership consisted of women.) He asserts that the Labour party has always represented a coalition of groups with different interests and this is what it should concentrate on now. The only viable strategy for the Left is to build alliances with non-class groups, the new social movements.

Hobsbawm thoughtfully points out that the Right often disarms the Left: the sharp point of discontent is broken by limited concessions by the Right. An example from American history is the New Deal, the policies of President Roosevelt's first administration 1933-7. The bourgeois revolutions, in Hobsbawm's view, created many new political institutions, but socialist revolutions have not on the whole, produced the institutions through which the needs of different groups can be expressed. A wide range of institutions and political debates are essential to socialism and socialists should be thinking about ways of developing them now. Democracy is not a luxury for socialism but is essential to it. We must not forget that the struggle for socialist hegemony must begin a long time before the gaining of power.

Let us now look deeper into the arguments that stress the making of negotiated alliances and coalitions in the name of the 'national-popular' or of some 'hegemonic' strategy.

The new social movements

Many thinkers have linked the rise of the new social movements — the women's movement, youth movements, anti-nuclear and peace movements, ecological movements and various urban or citizen movements — with changes in the mode of production. (During the last few years, for example, there has been a growth in large-scale structural unemployment, expansion of nuclear power, the rise of nuclear technologies and so on.) The new movements are often anti-bureaucratic, anti-industrial political forces. They have successfully broadened the struggle to something 'wider' than class politics. They want to universalize the issue of emancipation beyond the particularistic interests of industrial workers.

Alberto Melucci believes that the new movements are not primarily oriented towards instrumental objectives such as the conquest of political power or state apparatuses but rather towards autonomy or independence *vis a vis* the system and the immediate satisfaction of collective drives.[20] Secondly, these movements reject the politics of representative delegation and have an enthusiasm for direct participation and direct action. Melucci notes, thirdly, that most of the new movements give a central place to the body and, through it, to an understanding of human beings as part of the natural world. He believes, fourthly, that the new movements tend to refuse mediation of their demands by the political system against which they have defined themselves. One of the features that unites the new movements is the resolutely non-negotiable nature of their demands.

Among the most influential of the new social movements are those that are based in the cities. Urban social movements tend to mobilize around three central goals: one, the struggles over the services provided by the state (for example, the struggle over the quality of educational opportunities for black children). This could be called *collective consumption*. There is the struggle over *cultural identity*. And, thirdly, there is *political self-management* — the attempt to win a degree of autonomy. Community organisations have tried to gain a degree of control over the processes which shape day to day experience (for example, local campaigns for police accountability).

Many of the new social movements rely on mass mobilization rather than mass membership and, as we have been reminded by Manuel Castells, the movements are precarious, fragile collectivities and they often lose their identity when they become institutionalized.[21] Most urban social movements do not seem to be agents of social change but rather 'symptoms of resistance to domination'.

Castells has put it in this way: when people find themselves unable to control the world, they simply shrink the world to the size of the community.

Castells, like Gorz, lays great stress on the decline of the workers' movement which has been apparent in inverse proportion to the rise of the new social movements. This decline has been hastened by the fact that the orthodox parties of the Left still privilege industrial workers. They still depend ultimately on a mystical view of the proletariat as a 'universal class' which in liberating itself is expected to liberate everybody.[22] This is like the view of André Gorz who has argued that Hegelian philosophy has constructed a mythologized proletarian ideal which can never be matched by the composite, fractured and heterogeneous actions of the empirical working class.[23] Gorz's political programme can be summarized thus: work less, consume better, reintegrate culture with everyday life.

But what has this discussion about the new social movements got to do with the struggle of black people? It has been observed that Gorz's post-industrial utopia contains many of the themes and preoccupations which have emerged spontaneously from the political culture of black Britain.[24] In Paul Gilroy's view the recent uprisings in Britain's inner cities had their origins in a social movement. Disorderly protests reflect the experiences of participants and, by conveying antagonism against the world as it is, they can be shown to embody a view of how participants would like it to be.[25]

Because there is an apparent decline in the workers' movements in Britain many people have rejected the priority of class struggle. Many blacks believe that the Labour party is racist and therefore some of them prioritize race and the autonomous struggle of the black community. Paul Gilroy, for example, asserts that the political languages of class and socialism have been so thoroughly discredited by Labourism at home, and 'actually existing socialism' abroad, that they may be completely beyond resuscitation.[26] In contrast, the struggles around race are only one example of the dynamism and cultural vitality of the neo-populist social movements. But what is the agent of historical change? The answer is unequivocal: the urban social movements. Gilroy believes that collective identities spoken through race, community and locality are, for all their spontaneity, powerful means to co-ordinate action and create solidarity.

Gilroy rightly makes it clear that anti-racism is not an adequate heading under which the content, scope and direction of black protest and self-organization can be assessed. Blacks have a variety of goals — not just the elimination of racist ideology. But, ultimately, Gilroy's main hope is the community. Community signifies for him not just a distinctive political ideology but a particular set of values and norms in everyday life: mutuality, co-operation, identification and symbiosis.

I am sceptical about all this. I think both the argument of autonomous black struggle based on the 'community', and the one about alliances with 'neo-populist' social movements are inadequate. Blacks, even when unified, form too small a group for effective political action. The 'community' is an inadequate, romantic notion; many men and women in the black community, like many white women, want the same opportunities as white, upper class men, but they do not want to change capitalist society itself.

It seems to me that many black communities still have not worked out their priorities. This may be because of differences within the communities themselves. Some blacks still see things in terms of nationality. 'I'm an Indian', 'He's a Pakistani', 'She's a Bangladeshi'. There are some blacks who see themselves in individual rather than collective terms. I am thinking particularly of the many successful, middle class or petit-bourgeois Asians (during the last decade their commercial progress in the UK has been spectacular) who are concerned that others see them as good, moral, respectable people. Since they accept the *status quo*, they neither question nor challenge the system.

The suggestion is often made that Blacks should make alliances with some of the 'neo-populist' social movements but these are often fragile, divisive, bourgeois, with a tendency to become institutionalized. What does the policy of making alliances entail? It means first of all that the main agent, traditionally the revolutionary party, has to change its usual role. Instead of being a vanguard party it has to become an open, 'democratic' party so that it can win support but this often means that it loses its principles because it has to make compromises. When there is a policy of making alliances with non-class groups such as radical feminists, gays, blacks, environmentalists, nuclear disarmers, animal liberationists and others, the question arises: to what extent can a political party go on compromising? What is one willing to sacrifice for the sake of support from liberals and social democrats? With whom do you *not* have alliances? And in a 'rainbow' coalition where does leadership reside?

The black people to whom I have been talking are politically aware that as they are only a minority in this country they must make alliances with other exploited groups such as the white working class. They know that this is an irony because they have experienced interpersonal racism from white workers, and institutional racism from their organisations. However, many blacks are aware of the contradiction that the white working class has also been exploited and that to reject it totally is an unviable strategy.

Chapter 10

Education and social change

Re-vision

We noted earlier how many working class youngsters don't see the point of going to school. School seems irrelevant and so it is not surprising that there is disaffection and disruption. Of course, some middle class pupils feel that school is limiting too, but their parents know how to retain their class advantages and to transmit the 'know-how' to their children.[1]

Problems in school include shortage of books and materials, disruptive pupils, overworked, underpaid and demoralized teachers. I believe that these problems are external manifestations of deeper structural problems in society. One of the main aims of education is the transmission of values and once the framework is shaken the reproduction of these values becomes problematic.

I have argued that the present crisis in education is the crisis of capitalism. As a response to the crisis the conservative government in Britain has begun to stress the idea of a shareowning social democracy, a 'popular' capitalism. (Sadly, it seems that even the Labour party has been influenced by these notions.) At the same time, there has been a marked shift towards authoritarianism in political institutions. In the past, policies were debated and decisions were made in parliament but now they are increasingly being made by inner-cabinet committees.

Look what has happened in education. The main functions of education: the integrative, the egalitarian, and the developmental, are contradictory.[2] After World War II these three contradictory functions were held together by the expansion of the economy. But now, because of the economic crisis, equality for all is no longer considered feasible. The conservative government wants to return to a grammar school system for a small elite. It wants to offer 'training' (perhaps in the new 'City Technical Colleges') to the upper working-class. For the lower working-class there are government training schemes, but most young people know that these schemes neither foster personal development nor provide training for real jobs. ('These schemes', commented one young lad, 'are like a revolving door.') In short, what is happening in education is the re-imposition of an hierarchical, elitist system.

In the past, egalitarianism was somehow connected with an expanding economy but now the economy is stagnating. The capitalist labour process cannot absorb all the young. The labour market has disappeared in the inner cities and there is mass youth unemployment. This means that a new social condition is emerging: youth dependency. What do you do if you are black, working class, live in the inner city, and there is no work?

There is not only a North/South divide but also a division between employed and unemployed in every large city in Britain.[3] Consider some of the effects of youth unemployment: by being unemployed the young are excluded from many aspects of working class culture; in the past, for example, the young learnt things on the job from their elders but this is no longer possible. Learning through the trade union is also blocked. Being unemployed also means exclusion from leisure activities. If you don't have a wage you can't go to discos. The young unemployed are even excluded from the facilities provided by the local state leisure centres and so forth. Inevitably there is a retreat into the home and a collapse into the experience of isolation and depression. In this situation most young people see the state as being irrelevant and/or hostile.

This may be a convenient point in the text to summarize the main themes and arguments of the book. I hope that the following resumé will provide you with an opportunity to reflect on your views about the issues raised.

Chapter 1, an introduction to the field of education, described some attempts to explain the failure of working class children. Two views of social class, the empirical and the marxist, were explained, and then some of the main theoretical approaches used in education were outlined and assessed. It was suggested that in spite of their great analytical power these approaches tend to neglect the dynamics of gender and race.

Chapter 2, therefore, focused on the differing conceptions of the relationship between class, gender and race. It was argued that the relationships between these dynamics are continually shifting and that they often produce uneven and contradictory effects. This discussion was then linked to the issue of how racism shapes the experience of black pupils in schools. The educational performance of black children indicates that teachers must be more aware that class, gender, and race inequalities are different and that the methods used in one context cannot be applied to parallel initiatives in other areas.

This raised the question: what is the most effective approach to adopt? Chapter 3 outlined the main features of the debate between the supporters of multicultural education and those of anti-racist education. The assumptions, characteristics, and aims of both perspectives were outlined and criticised. It was argued that the controversial split between multiculturalists and anti-racists is actually an ideological struggle about the type of society in which we want to live.

To exemplify some of the points in the controversy between multicultural and anti-racist education, and to illustrate the ethnocentrism of the curriculum, Chapter 4 focused on one school subject: art. I showed how people are socialized into an ethnocentric view of art and culture through the organization of museums and the discourse of art history. European art is seen as an expression of civilization; non-European art equals primitivism. An outline of the development and ideological fuction of art in Westrern societies was followed by an analysis of the conflict between the supporters of the (traditional) 'ethnic arts' and the (politically aware) 'black arts'. This led to some reflections on the identity and role of black artists in contemporary Britain. The final section linked these discussions with art education and provided some examples of good practice in schools.

Many ideologies are used to prevent workers from perceiving their common exploitation. Chapter 5 began with an introduction to the concept of ideology. It was argued that ideologies are used to mislead and divert black people. Next came an examination of some of the ideologies ranged against them: the discourse of 'racial prejudice' in social psychology, 'equal opportunities', and 'ethnicity'.

But besides these, I argued, we also have to study the ideological discourse of imperialism, if we are fully to understand the structures of racism. Chapter 6 consisted of an examination of two key works by Frantz Fanon and Edward Said. Both texts (*Black Skin, White Masks* and *Orientalism*) are concerned, in their different ways, with cultural domination. These writings remind us of the importance of analysing imperialism and its psychological, social and economic effects. As education plays an important role in the maintenance of inequalities, the effects of imperialist rule on the education systems of so-called 'Third World' countries were considered.

Chapter 7 dealt with the ideology of nationalism. It was argued that the concept of 'the national past' has excluded the contributions of black people, and that the discourse of 'the nation' rejects black people by defining them as 'alien'. After a discussion of contemporary conservatism and its assumptions, there was an analysis of how 'Powellism' has characterized the black presence as a threat. The chapter concluded with a discussion of a current educational controversy, about the role of schools and parental choice, and the way in which many white parents see the presence of black pupils as a problem.

Chapter 8 continued the exploration of nationalism, national culture and identity and their inter-connections with 'race'. It analysed the radical shift to the Right in education, and argued that the attack on multicultural and anti-racist education was ideologically prepared. It considered the views and suppositions of some 'New Right' educationalists, in particular those associated with *The Salisbury Review* who privilege 'the nation' and believe in the superiority of British culture. Current government education proposals testify to the influence which the 'New Right' educationalists have achieved in government policy making. The chapter concluded with a discussion on the national curriculum and the effects it will have on black pupils.

But what were the theoretical processes by which the discourse of education was shifted to the Right? How has the Right's education policy won consent from so many people? One way of attempting to answer such questions is through the study of Gramsci's work, which is centrally concerned with the 'struggle over meaning'. Chapter 9 offered an introduction to Gramsci's thought and his views on hegemony and ideology. Recent developments in the theory of ideology by Althusser and Laclau were then explained. These developments are controversial because some theorists contend that class struggle is now of little importance. Laclau and others stress not class struggle but the making of alliances with a broad range of groups/movements in a 'popular-democratic' struggle. There was a discussion of how intellectuals like Stuart Hall and Eric Hobsbawm have used Gramsci's concepts to analyse the present political situation. The chapter concluded with a discussion about the new social movements and raised strategic questions about the future of black struggle.

Chapter 10 contains some positive suggestions for future policy and practice. It includes some concrete proposals that a socialist government should carry out and outlines some general principles (or injunctions) which could be the basis of a new politics of education. These 'injunctions' include a redefinition of 'really useful knowledge' for our time, the construction of a 'critical curriculum' that attempts to unite mental and manual labour, and the propagation of a new awareness of 'history' which includes the demystification of historical texts and the restoration of historical memory. I argue that being able to narrate your own history is very important and that story telling is a way of reappropriating the past. Telling the story of your loss is to reclaim it. I believe that in telling your own story you change your life — in naming it you make something new. Schools must provide — and enlarge

— public 'spaces', opportunities, facilities for the understanding of experience. The book will conclude with some reflections on education and popular planning.

The future: what should teachers do?

At a time when the government looks at the manifestations of the crisis but ignores the fundamental underlying problems, what should teachers do? What practical measures can we take? Here are some recommendations — some positive suggestions for future policy and practice.

The first thing we must do, of course, is to deconstruct our stereotypes. Afro-Caribbean pupils are often labelled outspoken, rude, rebellious, promiscuous and domineering. In contrast, are Asian pupils really passive and silent? In some classrooms whites dominate and we must check that the blacks are not being excluded. Are Asian girls being 'talked over' by white girls? And are black pupils having to translate the elaborate code of middle-class teachers?

Teachers must examine classroom materials and analyse them with their pupils. Textbooks contain many stereotypical images which affect how we 'see' and influence our behaviour and expectations.[4] What are the basic values and assumptions behind the representations? Black girls, for example, are usually depicted differently from white girls. But black girls do not form a homogeneous category; there are differences of age, class, religions and culture. Black pupils feel strongly about the prevalence of negative images in textbooks. Many teachers have responded and have worked hard to construct new materials.[5] But I believe that presenting positive images, with which black pupils can identify, is not enough. As I argued earlier, *an exclusive concern with the representation of blacks leaves the norm intact.* You will remember that I said that the school curriculum is ethnocentric — it celebrates England and Englishness — and argued that the discourse of the nation has become obsolete. It is the norm of 'Englishness' that we must begin to analyse and explore with our students to see how it has been constructed.[6]

Let me develop this point briefly. The question could be asked: is the racial Other the negative required by the white subject? Some white discourses situate black people outside representation. In other discourses blacks are negative, absent, lesser persons. In Western countries black culture is repressed — it returns only in certain 'acceptable forms'. As Fanon pointed out, black people are given the choice of either remaining silent, or of enacting the representation of themselves as lesser persons.

Many teachers and others have worked hard on analysing representations of black people in school books (and the media) and have looked at ways of substituting negative images with positive ones. While this is an important aspect of breaking down racist stereotypes, an exclusive concern with the representation of blacks (the white person's Other) leaves the 'norm' unchanged.

What is the 'norm'? The norm, I would argue, is the ideology of 'Englishness'. I suggest that we should focus on constructions of 'Englishness'in order to analyse what 'Englishness' is, whose 'Englishness' is dominant, and to look at how this dominant construction presents itself as natural and neutral.[7] This construction, this norm of 'Englishness', has a strategic function: it is able to absorb, contain and define all those outside it.

We are all concerned with the question: how should we live? We are constantly haunted by the discrepancy between what the world is like and what it could be like. I know some young philosophers who are advocating a society based on *difference*, a society in which people coming from different backgrounds and cultures can live peaceably together. They argue that the Western tradition has always stressed 'the same' rather than 'alterity'. Many people in Britain emphasize identity but the trouble with this is that it excludes difference. When I ask my friends what is the principle that would hold society together, they reply: 'The principle of difference, the agreement to honour difference. What we should do is to create a society where differences are cherished.' But is a society based on the principle of difference without hierarchy possible?

My guess is that these philosophers have been influenced by some French post-structuralist thinkers who are antagonistic to the Enlightenment project because they say that it effaced difference.[8] I think the above view is philosophically idealist because it does not take account of power. It assumes that a society based on hierarchy can, by mutual consent, be transformed to a society where the main value is difference.

Nevertheless, I think there is an important point here. The agreement to honour difference is better than its elimination. Sadly, at times in the past, the elimination of difference has been seen as essential to the creation of an ideal state, a state in which sameness was valorized. I think we would all agree that racism, which is really the condemnation of Otherness (or difference), does not merely victimize the Other. As a Lacanian psychoanalyst has put it, 'those who attempt to erase cultural difference, who wish to create a society in which Otherness is non-existent, come to be alienated from their own desire since this desire is the desire of the Other.'[9]

I am often asked by exasperated whites 'Well, what are the needs of black people? What do you want?' I have to reply that we wish to have equal treatment in schools, to gain access to higher education, to acquire skills and credentials, and to develop our sense of identity and culture. In my view, the struggle by blacks to gain these rights will mean an advance, an enrichment, for white people as well.

I believe that there must be more black involvement in education — as *students, parents, governors, teachers*. But it should be remembered that a black teacher is not just a teacher that happens to be black. And a 'black school' is not just like a white school with black pupils. I believe that a concerted attempt must be made to explain an unfamiliar education system to black parents; there must be full discussion with them about all aspects of the education of their children.

The training and employment of more black teachers would greatly help these processes. There are some people who understandably argue that blacks should not enter a deeply conservative teaching service whose main function is social reproduction. If it is a form of social control are not teachers in the job of 'soft policing'? My own view is that neither the police nor teachers are inherently bourgeois; both 'law and order' and 'education' are sites of class struggle. I think that black people should join both the police and the teaching services and (in spite of the risks and dangers of incorporation) try and use the contradictions in the institutions to alter them from within.[10] I would argue that though schools are a class instrument for the purpose of social reproduction, control and 'soft policing', they can *also* be a progressive, liberating force. Some teachers do manage, under very difficult conditions, to educate some of their students and raise their political awareness.

It is about time that administrators, educationalists and others started listening to what black teachers have to say. It is strongly felt by black teachers throughout the country that they are being barred from senior posts, and are being prevented from influencing the ways schools are run. This is an example of blatant inter-personal racism by white educationalists who should be fighting it.

Black teachers are concerned about the widening gulf between the school and the home. Many of them believe that schools *create* barriers in communication. Asian pupils in secondary schools have not been given a free choice to study the languages they want. They have often been forcibly put in European language groups. Now, one of the ten foundation subjects in the national curriculum is a modern foreign language: French, German, Spanish, Russian, but also, for pragmatic reasons, Arabic and Japanese. Asian or African languages are not even mentioned. Why should a European language be made compulsory for black pupils? Surely it would be more useful for black students to learn their community languages (unless, of course, the parents indicated the contrary)?

It is important that community languages be put on to the school timetable as early as possible — if the learning of a community language begins at 14 years of age it is too late — and in such a way that no Asian child is deprived of any 'essential' or career subject. Asian languages should be given equal standing to European languages and their status ought to be recognized by British examining bodies so that Asian children will not suffer in getting admission to higher education.

It seems to me that, if it is to be successful, *anti-racist education must concern itself with the social practices and cultural preoccupations of youth.* For many young people, working class youth and blacks, the experience of the street and the family may be becoming more important than the school (and what it tells — or provides). I want to suggest that in this situation *innovative youth work* with young people could be very productive. In such a context young people could learn to analyse lived culture, use new technology to develop their interests and investigate the new culture industries, and explore alternative forms of theorizing.

I think that supplementary schools, schools which are a direct response to the failure of the state to provide adequately for the educational needs of particular groups of children, should be encouraged. They could perhaps provide a new model of partnership between school and community. It is time we began looking at the ways in which schools could redefine their roles within the community. Schools, in short, must begin to reflect the concerns and needs of pupils *and* parents.

Many black parents are realizing that culture can be a powerful resource for change. They think that children are denied knowledge of their history and culture. Many parents feel that it is very important that black writers, actors, painters, singers and others regularly visit and work with students in the schools. Blacks must reappropriate their culture and not allow it to be commodified.

It is in the interest of teachers to keep educational debates alive. Whenever merely 'technical solutions' are expounded we must point out their inadequacy. As the state education system is under increasing strain, we should try and foster an interest in alternative, socialist views of education. The work of Paulo Freire, for example, could be useful in thinking about the issue of 'People's Education'.

I think that Paulo Freire's approach, consisting of analyses and discussions on certain key themes, could form an important part of anti-racist education: "What do we see here? What are these people doing?' the co-ordinator asks.

They are working with clay, the participants answer. 'They are changing the materials of nature with work', many answer.[11] And so Freire goes on, working away at his discussion-themes which include: the process of transforming nature, the value of human labour, labour and capital, manual and mental labour, wealth and poverty, the developed and the 'underdeveloped' nations, emancipation and world peace.

It is clear that the struggles in education must be linked with struggles in the community. Moreover, we must try and make our students more aware of the struggles of the oppressed peoples of the 'Third World'. In the past there was often a nostalgic, idealized view of these places. This must change. There is much to be learnt from the struggles in Africa and Latin America, and how these struggles are inter-connected. There must be a positive relation to the new, emerging countries and teachers can do much to foster this through the teaching of development and peace studies. This brings us to issues about the curriculum.

A 'critical curriculum'

It is vitally necessary to develop a new pedagogical political culture. In the rest of this chapter, therefore, I suggest some educational reforms that the government should carry out and outline some general principles which could be the basis of a 'critical curriculum' in an education system that stresses co-operative, collaborative and collective methods of learning and living.

One of the main tasks of teachers and parents is to demand the right to participate in the construction of a curriculum which will give young people confidence, social, political and economic competencies, knowledge and skills whereby young people can learn how to control their lives. Teachers must participate in the creation of a new anti-racist curriculum that is global, relevant and up-to-date. Even in a period when the state is beginning to tighten its control of the curriculum, much can still be done by teachers, collectively, at the level of the school. These changes will be ineffective however, unless there are changes in the examination system which, as is presently constituted, is a serious constraint on curriculum content. It is imperative that the examination boards consider questions of ethnocentric bias and of white cultural assumptions not only in curricula but in examinations. The increased representation of blacks on examination boards is highly desirable so that examinations reflect the multicultural society in which they take place. But the strategy of gaining educational qualifications does not go far enough. We know that when black people gain high qualifications they are still discriminated against.

There is, then, a lot to be done. Besides developing materials for one's own use, it is important to construct a syllabus which looks at issues from a multicultural perspective. This means not only finding ways of validating aspects, features and qualities that whites have suppressed, but also showing the full range of what black people have achieved.

Note that I said a multicultural perspective. A syllabus based on a black perspective could be seen as merely a 'reversal' of a white perspective. On the other hand, a model based on a synthesis would mean some sort of eclecticism and that would also be inadequate. We have, in the long run, to go beyond these sorts of binary oppositions. Ultimately, we need to transcend (*aufebung* in Hegel's terminology) these polarities and create a new type of curriculum.

In the past, curriculum theorists have tended to ignore discussion about the nature of society and the educational and social policies necessary to change it. At the same time there has been a lack of any significant practical or policy orientation in much radical sociology of education. I see no organic relationship between such work and political groups of the Left. Let me now outline some general principles, or rather injunctions, which concern the usefulness of 'equal opportunity' initiatives to raise class issues; the redefinition of 'really useful knowledge' for our time; the construction of a curriculum that attempts to unite mental and manual labour and emphasizes the restoration of historical memory.

The aim of the critical curriculum is the reverse of the traditional curriculum which 'naturalizes' events; it is to press students to question attitudes and behaviour which they have taken as 'natural'. Such a curriculum posits the view that reality is a changing, discontinuous process produced by human beings and so transformable by them. The task of the curriculum is not to 'reflect' a fixed reality but to reflect on social reality; it is to demonstrate how knowledge and social events are historically produced and so how they could have been, and still can be, different.

Within this new set of social relations, teachers would engage in critical reflection on their lessons in the act of teaching. And students would be encouraged to pass judgments on the performance and actions of teachers. It is important that students should feel that learning something new every day is exciting and enjoyable.[12] There should be an emphasis on fun. Learning is hard work but also very satisfying. The critical curriculum, then, focuses on the forms, not merely the contents of learning. I believe that though some teachers do manage to criticize society through the contents of the curriculum, their teaching often becomes socially ineffective because of the form. Just as in the history of art aestheticism stressed artistic autonomy, so similarly in the history of education the ideological notion of 'education for its own sake' has been very pervasive amongst certain 'liberal' philosophers of education. Ever since the institutionalization of schooling by the state, education has become more and more separated from life. Schools at present tend to reproduce and legitimize the division between mental and manual labour, and that is one of the reasons learning takes place in institutions divorced from daily life and experience.

Working-class groups, blacks and women have gained little of value from the traditional curriculum. So much of the academic curriculum still derives from the cultural experience of a ruling minority that vast numbers of pupils find little in it that is meaningful and that they can relate to. During the last few years there has been a trend towards vocationalism, even within schools, fostered by the Manpower Services Commission (MSC). The government justifies prevocational education by an appeal to industrial 'relevance', but the trouble is that it emphasizes training rather than thought and it has a completely uncritical approach to the status quo. Support for MSC initiatives stems from the way they exploit real deficiencies in secondary schooling, while doing nothing to remedy them.[13] Many of its courses have the effect of making existing forms of work and work discipline appear 'natural' rather than demonstrating the extent to which they are the product of a fundamentally unjust and inegalitarian society. I would argue, that the MSC is a colonizing institution and that its main purpose is social control of the young.

What should be done about the government's new vocationalism? There is no doubt that more attention needs to be paid to the development of alternatives that might have some appeal to the Left. The MSC, a powerful force in redefining education, has preconceptions of relevance that are very different from those of most educators. I suggest that rather than just accepting its definitions, we should try to redefine its schemes from an educationalist rather than a vocational point of view. Attempts should be made to develop with school-leavers an alternative approach to education that differs both from conventional social-studies practice and the social-and-life-skills ideology being fostered by the government with official TUC support. Attempts should be made to develop a pedagogy based upon the students' sense of priorities but which also challenges the students' tendency to accept the transition from school to unemployment as an individual rather than a collective problem.[14]

I believe that one of the crucial changes required is that schools should be integrated with production and the wider society. Now, you may say that the Right also want to bring learning and labour together. But the important difference is this: whilst the Right tend to think of schooling for the masses in terms of a limiting and restrictive training for manual labour, socialists must struggle for an education and society based on the dialectical unity of mental and manual labour.

I know that this struggle is particularly difficult at the present time: anything theoretical is being attacked, political education is under suspicion, Peace Studies, for example, has been removed from some schools; antiracist and antisexist initiatives are being limited rather than extended; control of education by the central government is tightening. This is the context in which teachers must work out for themselves the nature of the 'political' and what they must do in the classroom. We know that in the past, people's experience was too often discounted. The important thing that teachers must now do is to link different areas of experience, the mental and the manual, the social and the economic, the past and the present. Young people must be educated in such a way that they have the confidence to say what is unsaid and to challenge the received views of dominant ruling groups.

Young people also need to learn that race, sex and class are forms of division and domination. Recent initiatives against different forms of discrimination , however limited, are valuable in raising people's consciousness of these issues. I suppose the fundamental question concerns the relationship between these dynamics: which is the most important? Some writers I know emphasize these three dynamics equally all the time, which I think leads to a somewhat mechanical approach. Many people are assiduously trying to theorize which dynamic is primary; but I believe that there cannot be one definite answer to this question. To focus on one dynamic does not necessarily imply that the other two are negated. In different historical periods and situations, one dynamic may be a more powerful determinant than the others. In my own work I have always tended to concentrate on class analysis and must admit that I am worried that in some 'equal opportunity' initiatives the dynamics may become an unquestioned 'Holy Trinity'. Here are some of my misgivings: Does the support of liberals and social democrats for antiracist and antisexist projects lead to the dilution of class analysis? With the constant addition of new dynamics such as 'age', 'nation', 'religion', is the class dynamic being driven out to the periphery? Already in some circles it is quite acceptable to be antiracist and/or antisexist, but class, a dangerous and explosive concept, is repressed; it is seen as rather 'old fashioned', not really respectable.

Of course, I know that students now coming up to university are no longer ignorant of recent theoretical developments. They are, in fact, not only conversant with it but sometimes have a sophisticated knowledge of it. But, unfortunately, there is a powerful tendency in education to ever greater compartmentalization and specialization. If we really want to make connections, it is important to stress interdisciplinary work. Working collectively, we must make alternative views available. Moreoever, we must present them responsibly. The first task (to use Raymond Williams' phrase) is to 'unlearn the inherited mode'. We must unlearn the forms into which we have been socialized by challenging the agencies that stress conformism. A possible second stage could be the development of the teaching of school subjects so that young people can see how specific works relate to the structures of society.

'Really useful knowledge': the teaching of history

I am sadly aware that the Left has failed to develop, in conjunction with the political constituencies whose interests it claims to represent, a sense of a present-day equivalent of what nineteenth-century radicals called 'really useful knowledge'.[15] Surely it should be possible to conceive of working-class education in terms different from the received models? It is vital for the Left to realize that the prevailing curriculum models will not serve the needs of the disadvantaged groups within society: the working class, blacks and women. We must try to construct a curriculum that combines relevance and rigour; a genuinely comprehensive curriculum needs to be both meaningful and critical.

One of the first things we must do is to widen the curriculum so that it deals with the vital issues which are at present largely ignored: the depletion of the world's resources, pollution and deforestation, the nature of technology and its effects, the role of the multinationals, the nuclear arms race, the threat of the destruction of all life on the planet. These are matters of serious concern to many young people.[16] Surely it is time that in every school there were multidisciplinary courses that linked peace studies, the problems of developing countries and ecological themes?

As an example of 'really useful knowledge' let us think for a moment about the teaching of history in schools. We could begin by examining its dominant assumptions. It is necessary, for example, to ask academics why they so often write history as if what actually happened could not have *not* happened. And why can they not find new ways of teaching history? Perhaps teachers should plan courses on the history of childhood or courses on the history of excluded groups: the poor, the oppressed and the colonized.

Hayden White has analysed how historical discourse is produced and how all such productions are inherently interpretive. He has theorised, in a most interesting way, about history as *writing*.[17] Basically, he argues that an historical text may be seen as a romance, tragedy, comedy or satire. Other

137

genres get subsumed under these dominant ones. There are different types of plot and ideology. A text can express, for example, an anarchist, conservative, liberal or socialist point of view. There is also the preferred mode of explanation to consider: is it mechanistic, organicist, formalist? The historian, in short, performs certain processes of selection and arrangement, producing forms of plot, explanation and ideology.

Interpretation enters into historiography in at least three ways: aesthetically (in the choice of narrative devices), epistemologically (in the choice of an explanatory paradigm), and ethically (in the choice of moral judgement or recommendation). Every historical text always exhibits these three levels, the aesthetic, the epistemological and the ethical. Furthermore, there are four tropes — metaphor, metonymy, synecdoche, and irony — which underlie and inform all materials in the historical field. Tropes constitute the latent level or deep structure of every text.

White has analysed how historical discourse is produced and how all such productions are inherently interpretive. Of course, there are many objections to White's theory. Are all historical texts regulated by a small set of tropes? Do the tropological modes really determine our paths of thinking? Nevertheless, I like the way White tries to demystify historical texts. I would argue that there should be courses available to allow all students to understand how historians construct forms of plot, explanation and ideology which is called 'history'.

I have long argued that youngsters should know about the economic and political systems in which they live and about their history. One of the main problems is how to get young people to seek out the truth beneath the surface of things, to make connections and to be critical. It is very hard to teach pupils the fact that the history books in the library are not history. History is not a matter of printed words but is something direct, practical and made by people. Many youngsters know how to work on a bike or a car, but how do you work on history? How do you convey to young people the idea that a real understanding of history only comes about through making it?

My reflections on history have been stimulated by the work of two important theorists in the Brechtian tradition, Oscar Negt and Alexander Kluge.[18] They argue that in contemporary societies there is a struggle for interpretative power and that the prevailing ideologies limit the means by which individuals understand their material experiences. They believe that the modern culture-industry robs individuals of 'languages' for interpreting self and world, by denying them the media for organizing their own experiences. Through the mass media there is an attempt to dominate cultural life;

but is it necessarily successful? Do people's experiences remain on the subliminal level or are they dealt with consciously?

Negt and Kluge have developed an important concept which they call 'the public sphere of production'. The phrase refers to the discourses and institutions that can provide individuals or social groups with a medium in which to deal with subliminally felt experiences and learn to interpret these experiences on a more or less conscious and critical level. Literature and storytelling have important functions because they provide the means for dealing with experiences by discussing them. They contend that only experience confirmed and corroborated through discussion and coped with as collective experience can be said to be truly experienced. In their view consciousness is the historically concrete production of meaning, and they believe that every historical situation contains ideological ruptures and offers alternatives of thought.

I agree with Negt and Kluge that one of the tendencies of late capitalist societies is the expropriation of languages and their substituion by abstract representations. One of the most serious problems we face is how to provide — and enlarge — public 'spaces', opportunities, facilities for the understanding of experience. I believe that young people should be given every opportunity to discuss things in *small groups*. Group discussions can be quite difficult; those unfamiliar with this sort of learning often say that discussions 'never get anywhere', they 'never lead to anything'. At present so much of what we feel and think is seen as a personal experience, something individual, private. In contrast with this it is suggested that experiences should be discussed collectively. People have different responses to experiences and different capacities to process them. But a critical curriculum would emphasize the sharing of experiences through talking, discussion, debate, drama, open forums. We need to teach children about co-operative, collaborative methods of learning and living. Young people need to realize that personal problems, relationships with parents, their fears and anxieties, are interrelated with social ones. Talks should not be limited to a short discussion after a class has finished reading a book, or made a visit to a theatre or an art gallery. There should be joint discussion between staff and students about all sorts of things including the nature of school experience, the organisation of the school, the selection and presentation of knowledge. What is 'really useful knowledge' at the present time? What does 'equal opportunities' mean? And how can they be practised in this school? How can the curriculum be based on the unity of mental and manual labour?

It is very important that we try to break out of the disciplinary ghettos in which as students and teachers we have been confined. Perhaps we can gain experience in fields such as journalism, photography, film, drama, so that we can expose the system of power that authorizes certain representations while blocking, prohibiting or invalidating others. Instead of non-interference and specialization there must be interference, crossing of borders and obstacles. We must make a determined attempt to restore historical memory; we could use photomontage, video and other techniques to tell other stories than the 'official' or ideological ones produced by the institutions of power.[19] We ought to recover a history of society and of education which hitherto has been misrepresented or rendered invisible. The crucial point of all this work is that it should be linked with ongoing political practice. We need to reopen a debate about issues such as education and popular planning.

Education for all

Many of my suggestions in the section above may seem unrealistic at a time when a crucial aspect of the government's elitist social policy is to increase centralized control over the *form, content and character of the education system* as a whole. As the crisis deepens there has been a shift towards the right, and conservative academics and intellectuals are becoming increasingly assertive. They express their power directly, without the pretensions of 'democratic' procedures. In this situation many people are realigning themselves with the radical Right. The reasons for this trend are complex. Many of the neo-conservative ideas now permeating Britain and being taken up by the new Right have their source in 'post-marxist' thought. An attempt is being made to popularize right-wing ideas in politics and education in order to legitimize the shift towards an increasingly inegalitarian and authoritarian society. This trend must be reversed.

At one time we all had a dream, a dream of education for all. It was generally admitted that it would be expensive but it was argued that it was necessary for a democratic society. Of course, the goal of open access has always entailed struggle. The educational sphere has always been an area of class struggle and conflict. Education has always been jealously guarded because it is irredeemably subversive. It is, after all, a source of power and pleasure.

It is difficult to achieve this aim in the present withering economic climate. Education is now under sustained attack from the state (increasingly involved in social reproduction) and its allies. There has been a rapid growth in a new educational philosophy which insists that education should be limited. And so there is a redefinition, a restructuring, of education; institutions are becoming increasingly hierarchical and there is a drive against critical knowledge. Some subjects are being axed and there is a rapid growth of mindless vocationalism.

Nevertheless, there is an enormous hunger and thirst for knowledge of all kinds. The sad fact is that many educationalists have stopped believing in the principle of education for all.[20] At a time when the 'New Right' has been exploiting the gaps and divisions among the Left many educationalists have colluded with the state. So far the Left, has done little to mobilize popular sentiments, to form the needs and desires of the new constituencies which will have to be organized through political work.

All this will have to change. Teachers will have to abandon old conceptions of professionalism and develop new ways of working within feminist, ecological, black and other movements. Education workers will need to be more actively involved in collective political movements at all levels. Oppositional interventions in and around education can play a significant role in social transformation when consciously linked with other groups committed to similar ends in other spheres. Policy will have to be developed from the grass roots, growing out of popular experience, not merely handed down by professional politicians and their professional educationalists. Moreoever, I believe that socialist parties should set up their own agencies of self-education; they themselves should be important centres of education.

When a socialist government is in power it should carry out the following educational reforms: Since inequality begins very early in the home there should be state nursery schools for all, where parental participation would be encouraged. Steps should be taken to incorporate the public schools into the state system, and payments made by commercial and industrial firms for the education of their employees' children should be made illegal. Much more help should be give to working-class pupils regarding educational choices and opportunities. Means should be found whereby the decision about the choice of examination subjects can be delayed. The government will have to think seriously about the educational facilities for girls, blacks and working-class children and review the 16-19 provision. There must be a much more positive approach to education. One of the first steps in this direction must be to seek ways of strengthening teachers' morale. And we must find ways of encouraging a community involvement in a popular education. One way of doing this is through popular planning.

At the present time many people are cynical about planning because they have experienced its oppressiveness. Most planning is by educational 'experts' who are out of touch with their clients; it is done by administrators and bureaucrats on behalf of others. Popular planning turns this positivist, impositional model upside down. Popular planning is about making a felt need into something explicit and concrete.

If the idea of popular planning were applied to education the first step would be to ask: what is it that people want from education? A list would be drawn up of equipment, facilities and skills available at each school, in each locality, and then plans drawn up by parents, teachers, pupils. This would be at the level of popular, community initiatives. It should then be possible to go to the state for financial help. This seems to me to be one way in which a public service could be made more accountable.

What are the counter-arguments? It could be argued that if people are asked what the educational system should provide, they may well suggest regressive policies and want an education that has reactionary aims. I believe that in a democracy this risk must be taken. At a time of rapid social change many parents feel insecure and tend to become rather conservative. On the other hand, the views of parents, pupils and teachers may well come as a surprise and, in some areas at least, may be in advance of the 'official' view. But, in any case, there would be safeguards. Popular planning need not always be populist. The point about having general principles is that they are used as criteria to determine actions and policies.

A second objection to popular planning is that teachers would feel reluctant about working with parents. Sadly, most teachers still feel self-conscious about the presence of others in their classrooms but such feelings should be overcome. I feel hopeful. Teachers are now coming to realize that they are not merely professionals but workers. In the past, many groups have talked about making the education system more open. The liberal view, for example, emphasizes this, but what I notice is that liberals never talk about inequalities of power. I want to argue that we must overcome the feeling of powerlessness that so many people feel. Power must return to the people.

These changes would go some way towards reaffirming our belief in the principle of equal education for all. A socialist society should develop its own curricula and pedagogies, its own definition of 'really useful knowledge'. In such a society education would be redefined as a strategy for changing not only the self but the world.

Notes and references

Chapter 1: Education and class

1   I wonder what the function of narrative is in our culture? What sort of story telling occurs in law courts, fairy stories, parliament, newspapers, television, schools? See Erich Auerbach, *Mimesis: The Representation of Reality in Western Literature,* Princeton, Princeton University Press, 1968.

2   Basil Bernstein, *Class, Codes and Control*: Volume 1, St. Albans; Paladin, 1973. For an introduction to the sociology of Bernstein see Paul Atkinson, *Language, Structure and Reproduction,* London, Methuen, 1985.

3   William Labov, 'The Logic of Non-standard English', in *Language and Education,* London, Routledge & Kegan Paul, 1972, p.198. Harold Rosen, *Language and Class,* London, Falling Wall Press,. 1972.

4   Samuel Bowles and Herbert Gintis, *Schooling in Capitalist America,* London, Routledge & Kegan Paul, 1976.

5   Paul Willis, *Learning to Labour: How working class kids get working class jobs,* London, Saxon House, 1977, p.3.

6   Ibid., p.3.

7   Ibid., p.96.

8   David Hargreaves, *The challenge for the comprehensive school: Culture, curriculum and community*, London, Routledge & Kegan Paul, 1982.

9   Stephen Wood,l (ed.), *The Degradation of work? Skill, deskilling and the labour process,* London, Hutchinson, 1982.

10 David McLellan (ed.), Karl Marx, *Selected writings*, Oxford, Oxford University Press, 1977 p.222. This is a very useful compilation.

11 Perry Anderson, *Arguments Within English Marxism*, London, Verso, 1980, p.55.

12 Geoffrey de Ste. Croix, 'Class in Marx's Conception of History', *New Left Review*, Number 146, July-August 1984, p.100.

13 See the booklet *Race, Sex and Class 1. Achievement in schools*, London, ILEA, 1983, p.7.

14 A.H. Halsey, et al., *Origins and destinations*, Oxford; Oxford University Press, 1980.

15 Ivan Reid, *Social class differences in Britain; a source book,* London, Open Books, 1977. pp. 164-196.

16 Michael F.D. Young (ed.), *Knowledge and control*, London, Collier Macmillan, 1971.

17 See Madan Sarup, *Marxism and education; a study of phenomenological and Marxist approaches to education*, London, Routledge and Kegan Paul, 1978.

18 Perhaps I ought to remind readers that Marx conceptualised a triadic structure: The economic base is material. It consists not only of the forces of production but the relations of production. The superstructure is both ideal and material. The relationship between the economic base and the superstructure is *dialectical*. And then there are ideas. This level is ideal; ideas remain impotent until they are translated into institutions and practices. See Karl Marx, Preface to *A Critique of Political Economy*, the section that begins: In the social production of their life, men enter into definite relations that are indispensable and independent of their will ....

19 Mechanical reductionism often leads to technological determinism — as in Kautsky and Bukharin.

20 Michael Apple 'Curricular form and the logic of technical control' in Michael Apple (ed.) *Cultural and economic reproduction in education,* London, Routledge & Kegan Paul, 1982.

21 Robert Bocock, *Hegemony*, London, Tavistock, 1986.

Chapter 2: Class, gender and race: black pupils in schools

1   A Sivanandan, *A Different Hunger: Writings on Black Resistance*, London, Pluto Press, 1982, p.93. He is a joint Editor of *Race and Class* which can be obtained from the Institute of Race Relations, 2-6 Leeke Street, London WC1 9HS. See also A. Sivanandan, *Communities of Resistance*, London, Verso, 1990.

2   John Rex and Sally Tomlinson, *Colonial Immigrants in a British City*, Routledge & Kegan Paul, London, 1979.

3   Sivanandan, in 1972, took over the white, prestigious Institute of Race Relations and turned it into a research and political centre of and for the victims of racism. See Chris Mullard, *Race, Power and Resistance*, London, Routledge & Kegan Paul, 1985.

4   J. Gabriel and G. Ben-Tovim, 'The conceptualization of race relations in sociological theory', in *Ethnic and Racial Studies*, Volume 2, Number 2, 1979.

5   The term 'popular-democratic' derives from a reading of Antonio Gramsci whose work is examined in Chapter 9.

6   Paul Gilroy, *'There Ain't No Black in the Union Jack': The cultural politics of race and nation*, London, Hutchinson, 1987, p.34, (my emphasis). This is a more sophisticated approach than the one he espoused in an earlier work: Paul Gilroy, et al., *The Empire Strikes Back: Race and racism in 70s Britain*, London, Hutchinson, 1982.

7   Robert Miles, Marxism versus the sociology of 'race relations'?, in *Ethnic and Racial Studies* Volume 7, Number 2 April 1984, p.217.

8   Miles writes that we should not ignore the group of migrants whose political ideology and practice is conservative. These 'black conservatives' are, for example, in favour of 'stricter standards' in school, Thatcherite 'enterprise' culture, and so on. We do not know how widespread such views are, or how they are reproduced. Many of these migrants may have some material interests in land or other forms of property in the country of their birth.

9   Miles, op.cit., p.229.

10 See the two Open University readers: Madeleine Arnot and Gaby Weiner, *Gender and the Politics of Schooling*, London, Hutchinson, 1987, and Gaby Weiner and Madeleine Arnot, *Gender under scrutiny*, London, Hutchinson, 1987.

11 See, for example, Juliet Mitchell and Jacqueline Rose (eds.), *Feminine Sexuality: Jacques Lacan and the ecole freudienne*, Macmillan, London, 1982.

12 While the general invisibility of women from historical accounts of struggle has been acknowledged by many White feminists, the absence of Black women has not been seen as being of any significance. To give just one

example, the resistance of Asian and Afro-Caribbean women to slavery and colonialism is often not mentioned in many history books. See Hazel Carby "White women, listen': black feminism and the boundaries of sisterhood', in Centre of Contemporary Studies, *The Empire Strikes Back*, op.cit.

13   Michel Foucault, 'Georges Canquilhem: philosopher of error', in *I & C*, 7, Technologies of the Human Sciences, 1980, p.54.

14   Perry Anderson, *In the Tracks of Historical Materialism*, London, Verso, 1983, p.92.

15   This 'finding' (of the Rampton Report, Cmnd. 8273, HMSO, 1981), raises the question: if both the 'West Indian' and 'Asian' communities are victims of racism, why is it that one group performs better than another? This may be an example of the creation of a new racial hierarchy based on a false division among the oppressed. See Godfrey Brandt, *The Realization of Anti-racist Teaching*, Lewis, The Falmer Press, 1986.

16   Brown and Brown, *White Britain*, Policy Studies Institute, 1984.

17   For an insightful study of Asian attitudes and educational aspirations, see Harwant Bains' 'Southall Youth: An Old-Fashioned Story' in Philip Cohen and Harwant Bains (eds.), *Multi-Racist Britain*, London, Macmillan, 1988. He is particularly insightful about the conservatism of Punjabi perspectives. Unfortunately, many Asians have been unable to identify with the rest of the Black community or the White working class.

18   In this section I am indebted to the research of Philip Cohen (ibid.).
See also Philip Cohen, *Tackling Common Sense Racism*: Annual Report 1988/89 of the Cultural Studies Project. This can be obtained from the Centre for Multicultural Education, Institute of Education, 20, Bedford Way, London, WC1H 0AL.

Chapter 3: Multicultural and/or antiracist education?

1 See Maureen Stone, *The Education of the Black Child in Britain*, London, Fontana, 1981.

2 James Lynch, 'The multicultural curriculum: some guidelines for action', in Louis Cohen and Alan Cohen (eds.), *Multicultural Education: A sourcebook for teachers*, London, Harper and Row, 1986, p.201.

3 Ellis Cashmore and Barry Troyna, *Introduction to Race Relations*, London, Routledge & Kegan Paul, 1983, p.35.

4 A famous study of prejudice stated that some people possessed an authoritarian personality. They tended to be anti-Semitic, anti- black, rigid in their beliefs and extremely suspicious of minority groups. Their values and attitudes stemmed from childhood experiences. See Theodor Adorno, et.al, *The Authoritarian Personality*, New York, Harper and Row, 1950.

5 In 1985 the European court of Human Rights unanimously held that United Kingdom immigration law was in breach of the European Convention on Human Rights. The law stated that foreign women married or engaged to men settled in the UK were entitled to join them in the UK, but foreign men had no right to join their wives or fiancees settled in the UK unless certain conditions were satisfied. For details of the racial basis of the UK's immigration laws see Ellis Cashmore, *Dictionary of Race and Ethnic Relations*, London, Routledge & Kegan Paul, 1984, p.122.

6 This thesis is developed more fully in Madan Sarup, *Marxism, Structuralism, Education*, London, Falmer, 1983.

7 Robert Jeffcoate, 'Combating Racism', in Louis Cohen and Alan Cohen (eds.) *Multicultural Education*, op.cit., p.48.

8 Ibid., p.51.

9 Sally Tomlinson, 'Multi-racial schooling: parents' and teachers' views', *Education 3-13*, Vol.9, No.1, pp.16-21.

10 Jeffcoate in Cohen and Cohen, op.cit., p.53. I would like to point out that a 1981 Home Office report showed that the rate of racial victimization for Asians was 50 times that for white people, and the rate for West Indians was over 36 times that for white people. See HMSO, *Racial Attacks*, London, HMSO, 1981.

11 A study on stereotyping found that though black and white pupils initiated contact with the (white) teacher about equally, the teacher clearly favoured the 'gifted' white pupils, followed by the 'non-gifted' whites, then the 'non-gifted' blacks and, last, the 'gifted' blacks. This experiment demonstrated a racial stereotyping so strong that ability is a positive quality in some teachers' eyes only if it is shown by a white pupil; an able black pupil is likely to have even more negative teacher contact than a slow one. See P.L. Rubovits and M.L. Maehr, 'Pygmalion black and white', *Journal of Personality and Social Psychology*, Vol. 25, No. 2, 1973, pp.210-18.

12   Jeffcoate in Cohen and Cohen, op.cit., p.66.

13   Ray Honeyford, in 'Black and White', in *The Salisbury Review*, January 1987, pp.64-66. This is a review of the book by Madan Sarup, *The Politics of Multiracial Education*, London, Routledge & Kegan Paul, 1986. All the quotations in this section are from the review.

14   Phil Cohen *'Anti-racist Cultural Studies: A curriculum development project in school and community education'*, unpublished, 1986.

15   The real reason for immigration at the end of the Second World War was that there was an (estimated) labour shortage of one million people. Most people believe the 'common-sense' story: for economic reasons black people came to Britain in the 1950s; the indiginous people were unhappy about this, and that the 'liberal' state was forced to pass laws restricting migration. Recent research, however, shows that the State constructed migration flows in particular ways and that the state actively constructed a racist environment to influence the electorate. The state collected statistics about black crime, etc., to justify its racist policies and to build populist support against the new black migrants. The irony is that it was the post-war Labour government, attempting to build socialism in a capitalist society, that was largely responsible. See Robert Miles, *Capitalism and Unfree Labour.*

16   Ernesto Laclau, *Politics and Ideology in Marxist Theory*, London, Verso, 1977, p.102. Laclau's theory of discourse will be discussed in Chapter 9.

Chapter 4: Racism and art

1   Alan Bullock and R.B. Woodings (eds.), *The Fontana Biographical Companion to Modern Thought*, London, Collins, 1983, p.598.

2   In this section I would like to acknowledge a borrowing from Tony Brown, Racism in Art History, *Multicultural Teaching*, Vol.5, No.2, Spring 1987, pp.32-35. This useful journal is obtainable from Trentham Books Ltd., Unit 13/14 Trent Trading Park, Botteslow Street, Stoke-on-Trent, Staffs., England ST1 3LY.

3   Two books that illustrate a Eurocentric approach to knowledge are E.H. Gombrich, *The Story of Art*, London, Phaidon, 1978, and Kenneth Clark, *Civilisation*, London, B.B.C., 1969.

4   George Steiner, *Language and Silence*, London, 1967.

5   Jorge Larrain, *The Concept of Ideology*, London, Hutchinson, 1979, p.50.

6   Peter Bürger, *Theory of the Avant-Garde,* Manchester, Manchester University Press, 1984, p.48.

7   Herbert Marcuse, 'The Affirmative Character of Culture', in *Negations*: essays in critical theory, Harmondsworth, Penguin, 1968.

8   Is exile dissidence? Kristeva considers exile as a necessary condition to attain to the irreligious state from which one would always be in opposition to any homogenization. Exiles, by being in the place where they are out-of-place, always represent a heterogeneous exception to the constitution of a homogenious group. See Julia Kristeva, 'A New Type of Intellectual: The Dissident' in Toril Moi (ed.), *The Kristeva Reader*, Oxford, Basil Blackwell, 1986, p.292.

9   Art and Development Education 5-16 Project is a three year Oxfam/ILEA curriculum development project. I wish to acknowldge the stimulus and support I have received from the project team: Janie Butler, Aileen McKenzie and Sonya Walters. For useful materials contact the Education Department, Oxfam, 274 Banbury Road, Oxford OX2 7DD.

10   Oliver Cromwell Cox, *Caste, Class and Race, A Study of Social Dynamics*, New York, Doubleday,1948.

11   A. Sivanandan, 'The Struggle for Black Arts in Britain', in *Race and Class*, Vol. XXVIII Summer 1986, No.1 p.77.

Chapter 5: Ideologies of racism

1   James Donald and Stuart Hall (eds.), *Politics and Ideology*, Milton Keynes, Open University Press, 1986, p.ix. See also John B. Thompson, *Studies in the Theory of Ideology*, Oxford, Polity Press, 1984.

2   Jorge Larrain, *The Concept of Ideology*, London, Hutchinson, 1979, p.210.

3   Lord Scarman, *The Brixton Disorders*, London, Penguin, 1982, para.4.63.

4   Julian Henriques, 'Social Psychology and the politics of racism', in Julian Henriques, et.al., *Changing the Subject: Psychology, social regulation and subjectivity*, London, Methuen, 1984. Henriques traces the development of the notion of prejudice from Adorno's work which recognized irrationality and its effects, through Allport's emphasis on the notion of inaccurate judgement, to Tajfel's cognitivist explanation of it as error based on arbitrary mistakes.

5   Theodor Adorno, et.al., *The Authoritarian Personality*, New York, Harper and Row, 1950. G.W. Allport, *The Nature of Prejudice*, New York, Addison Wesley, 1954.

6   That Britain is a racist society is a proposition that Lord Scarman does not accept. He writes 'It was alleged by some of those who made representations to me that Britain is an institutionally racist society. If by that is meant that it is a society which knowingly, as a matter of policy, discriminates against black people, I reject the allegation. If, however, the suggestion being made is that practices may be adopted by public bodies as well as by private individuals which are unwittingly discriminatory against black people, then this is an allegation which deserves serious consideration, and, where proved, swift remedy.' Lord Scarman, op.cit., para.2.21.

7   A. Sivanandan, 'RAT and the degradation of Black struggles', *Race and Class,* 26/4.

8   The Commission for Racial Equality has recently accused education authorites of dragging their feet on 'widespread and persistent' racial harassment in schools. The commission said that only 47 out of 115 local education authorities had published or were working on guidelines on racial harassment. See *The Guardian*, March 30, 1988. The report *Learning in Terror* can be obtained from CRE, Elliot House, 10 Allington Street, London SW1E 5EH.

9   This is according to an independent report commissioned by the new Labour administration in the London Borough of Ealing. This report came the day after the influential Runnymeade Trust found that job prospects remain unchanged twenty years after the Race Relations Act was passed. See *The Guardian*, March 16, 1988.

10 John Stone, *Racial Conflict in Contemporary Society*, London, Fontana Press/Collins, 1985, p.35.

11   Anthony Smith, *The Ethnic Origins of Nations*, Oxford, Basil Blackwell, 1986.

12   Julia Kristeva, *Desire in Language; A Semiotic Approach to Literature and Art*, Oxford, Basil Blackwell, 1981, p.111.

Chapter 6: Racism and imperialism

1   Frantz Fanon, *Black Skin, White Masks*, London, Pluto Press, 1986. This edition contains a foreword by Homi Bhabha.

2   Ibid., p.74.

3   Ibid., p.76.

4   Ibid., p.177.

5   Ibid., p.162.

6   Ibid., p.83-108. This chapter is a critique of Octave Mannoni, *Prospero and Caliban: The Psychology of Colonization*, New York, Prager, 1964.

7   Négritude is a term coined by French black intellectuals to express the sense of common Negro inheritance and destiny. Poets such as Aimé Césaire and Leopold Senghor emphasized the rediscovery of one's past, one's culture, one's ancestors and one's language. Négritude was an attempt to create an African consciousness for blacks wherever they were; it instilled black people with a sense of history and culture but it lacked a political dimension.

8   Fanon, op.cit., p.133.

9   This section shows the influence on Fanon of Lacanian theory. See Jacques Lacan, *Family Complexes*, Oxford, Basil Blackwell, 1986.

10 According to Jung non-Europeans are primitive, have no history, exist in an emotional morass, have no will or thought. See Farhad Dalal, 'The racism of Jung', in *Race and Class,* Volume XXIX, Number 3, Winter, 1988.

11 G.W.F. Hegel, *The Phenomenology of Mind*, London, 1931. See also Richard Norman, *Hegel's Phenomenology: A Philosophical Introduction*, Sussex University Press, 1976, pp.46-66.

12 Edward W. Said, *Orientalism*, London, Penguin Books, 1985, p.327.

13 Ibid., p.40.

14 Karl Marx, *Surveys from Exile*, ed. David Fernbach, London, Penguin Books, 1973, pp.306-7.

15 Said, op.cit., p.206.

16 Said, op.cit., p.322.

17 Fanon, op.cit., p.IX.

18 For a poststructuralist reading of Fanon and Said see Homi Bhabha, 'The Other Question ...' *Screen,* Vol. 24, No.6, Nov-Dec 1983.

19 Frantz Fanon, *The Wretched of the Earth*, New York, Grove Press, p.93.

20 Anthony Wilden, *System and Structure*, London, Tavistock, p.478.

21 Robert Irwin, 'Writing about Islam and the Arabs', *Ideology and Consciousness,* winter 1981-2. But see also Edward Said, 'Orientalism Reconsidered' in *Race and Class*, Autumn 1985.

22 M. Carnoy, *Education as Cultural Imperialism*, David McKay, 1974. However, some writers have suggested that these 'dependency' theories lead to an over-deterministic relationship between schooling and the economy, and underestimate the possibilities of resistance or of the creation of alternatives in the pattern of schooling.

23 In Victorian Britain the middle class had a great fear of the moral, social and political contamination from the masses. It was in this situation that the ideological apparatuses of the State, the Church, the charitable institutions, the (elementary) schools intervened. Teachers were to bring culture and civilization to the people. They were to be agents of 'sweetness and light' (in Matthew Arnold's phrase), to elevate the working classes to culture. In this process it was assumed that culture would be the solvent of class antagonism, that 'culture' would do away with classes altogether. See Gerald Grace, *Teachers, Ideology and Control*; A study in Urban Education, London, Routledge & Kegan Paul, 1978.

24 Philip Altbach and Gail Kelly (eds.) *Education and Colonialism*, New York, Longman, 1978. See also V.G. Kiernan, *Marxism and Imperialism*, London, Edward Arnold, 1974; Anthony Brewer, *Marxist Theories of Imperialism*: A Critical Survey, Routledge, 1980.

Chapter 7: Racism and 'the nation'

1   See Patrick Wright, 'A Blue Plaque for the Labour Movement? Some political meanings of the 'National Past'', in *Formations of Nation and People*, London, Routledge & Kegan Paul, 1984.

2   Jurgen Habermas, *Legitimation Crisis*, London, Heinemann Education Books, 1976.

3   See Patrick Wright, *On Living in an Old Country: The National Past in Contemporary Britain*, London, Verso, 1985.

4   I draw here on Philip Cohen, 'The Perversions of Inheritance: Studies in the Making of Multi-Racist Britain' in Philip Cohen and Harwant Bains (eds.), *Multi-Racist Britain*, London, Macmillan, 1988.

5   Quoted in Benedict Anderson, *Imagined Communities: Reflections on the Origin and Spread of Nationalism*, London, Verso, 1983, p.86.

6   Ibid., p.136. Anderson claims that racism is essentially antithetical to nationalism because nations are made possible in and through print languages rather than notions of biological difference and kinship.

7   Philip Cohen, op.cit., p.64.

8   Benedict Anderson, op.cit., p.15.

9   Hugh Cunningham, 'The Language of Patriotism, 1750-1914', *History Workshop*, No.12, Autumn, 1981.

10   Bhikhu Parekh, 'The New Right and the Politics of Nationhood' in *The New Right: Image and Reality*, The Runnymede Trust, 1986.

11   Ibid., p.34.

12   In this context note the ideological role of *sociobiology*. Basically, this is an extension of Darwin's evolutionary theory as applied to animal and particularly human behaviour. It is argued that in order to preserve their genetic inheritance individuals will cooperate with each other in proportion to the degree to which they are biologically related. Thus human cooperation and apparent 'altruism' can be explained in terms of genetic selfishness. A biological basis for ethnocentrism and racism is attributed to an extended version of this process of kin selection which includes not just the family and close relatives, but also tribes, ethnic groups, 'races' and nations.

13   For some important essays on the state, nationalism and colonialism see David Held et.al. (eds.), *States and Societies,* Oxford, Martin Robertson, 1983.

14   Enoch Powell, speech at Eastbourne, 16-11-68, quoted in Paul Gilroy *'There Ain't No Black in the Union Jack': The cultural politics of race and nation,* London, Hutchinson, 1987, p.46.

15   Raymond Williams, *Towards 2000*, Harmondsworth, Pelican, 1983.

16   Ibid., p.195.

17   Peregrine Worsthorne, *Sunday Telegraph*, 27.6.82. For a socialist view on the war over the Falklands see Anthony Barnett, 'Iron Britannia', *New Left Review,* Number 134, July-August, 1982.

18   Eric Hobsbawm, in *Marxism Today*, January, 1983. The concept of hegemony is discussed fully in Chapter 9.

19   Ray Honeyford's articles can be found in *The Salisbury Review*, summer 1983, winter 1984, and January 1987.

Chapter 8: The New Right, 'race' and education

1   One of the best books on this period is the one produced by a group from the Centre for Contemporary Studies, *Unpopular Education: Schooling and social democracy in England since 1944*, London, Hutchinson, 1981, p.65.

2   Ibid., pp.200-207.

3   Ibid., pp.208-215.

4   The government's assisted-places scheme is mainly for extra- bright children. There are now 28,000 children on assisted places at private schools in England and Wales, and a further 3,000 in Scotland. Their fees are paid, wholly or partly, by the government. *The Sunday Times,* 15 May, 1988.

5   What follows is based on an article by Laurence Budge, The 'Salisbury Review': A Study in the Discourse of Neo-Conservatism, *Block 13*, 1987/8, p.69.

6   Jonathan Savery, 'Anti-Racism as Witchcraft', *The Salisbury Review*, July, 1985.

7   The text of the Prime Minister's address to the General Assembly of the Church of Scotland can be found in *The Guardian*, Monday 23rd May, 1988.

8   *Living in Terror,* published by the Commission for Racial Equality, Elliot House, 10/12 Allington Street, London SW1E 5EH.

9   See *The Times,* Monday May 16, 1988, p.3.

10 Antony Flew, *Education, race and revolution*, London, Centre for Policy Studies, 1984.

11 Ray Honeyford, in *Times Educational Supplement,* 19th November, 1982.

12 Geoffrey Partington, in *Police,* August, 1982.

13 Ray Honeyford, 'Education and race — an alternative view', *Salisbury Review,* Winter, 1984.

14 The inquiry team was led by Mr Ian Macdonald, QC. See *The Guardian*, Tuesday, May 10, 1988.

15 *ILEA News,* 19 May, 1988, p.14.

16 For examples of the New Right campaign against anti-racist education see Frank Palmer (ed.), *Anti-racism: an assault on education and value*, London, Sherwood Press, 1986. It contains articles by Flew, Honeyford, Scruton and other contributors to the *Salisbury Review.*

17 Paul Gordon, 'U.K. Commentary: The New Right, race and education — or how the Black Papers became a White Paper', *Race and Class*, Volume XXIX, Winter 1988, Number 3, p.95.

18 Berkshire's new Conservative administration has recently tried to abandon its anti-racist and multicultural policy statement. Kensington and Chelsea have announced that it would abandon the ILEA's policies on ethnic mi-

norities and adopt a 'colour blind' policy when it gains control of its schools. See *The Guardian*, Tues. 5 April, 1988, p.21.

19   Some facts about the independent sector: the 560,000 children at 2,500 fee paying schools total more than 7 per cent of the United Kingdom school population, compared with 5.8 per cent 10 years ago. Fees for boarders averaged £5,685 at the leading public schools and £4,300 at preparatory schools. The average pupil-teacher ratio is 11.6:1. *The Times*, Wed. 27 April, 1988, p.3.

20   S. Pearce, 'Education and the multiracial society', Policy Paper no.1, R4, London, The Monday Club, 1985. Both quotations are in Martin Francis, 'Issues in the fight against the Education Bill', *Race and Class,* Winter 1988, p.105.

21   Angela Rumbold, *The Sunday Times*, 22 Nov., 1987.

22   Kenneth Baker, *The Times Educational Supplement*, 25 Sept., 1987.

23   *Educational Worker*, June 1927, quoted in Ken Jones, *Beyond Progressive Education*, London, Macmillan, 1983, p.23.

24   The ideologies of Englishness have long been linked to the expansion of empire. A range of new and forceful national identities was produced, organized not only in the state and political institutions but throughout the civil order itself. For essays on the varied forms in which Englishness was constructed and reproduced see Robert Colls and Philip Dodd (eds.), *Englishness, Politics and Culture 1880-1920,* London, Croom Helm, 1986.

25   The important question of slavery is not often discussed in the history of colonialism. It is clear that chattel slavery became an obstacle to capitalism and that wage-labour became much more profitable. The anti-slavery movement may have granted freedom to the slave but, ironically, it may have helped to bind the wage labourer to capital even tighter. Wilberforce and other social reformers appear liberatory but, in a way, they also created new forms of imprisonment. Throughout this period there was a pervasive notion that the European had fuller rights. The Declaration of Rights was written by Thomas Jefferson, and other Virginian slave owners who argued that chattel slavery should be continued. The first declaration of freedom for slaves in 1794 was an outcome of the French Revolution. See Robin Blackburn, *The Overthrow of Colonial Slavery 1776-1848, London, Verso, 1988.*

26   C. MacNeil, 'The National Curriculum: A Black Perspective', *Multicultural Teaching,* Vol. 6, No.2.

27   In a lecture entitled 'Jane Austen and Empire', University of London, 9th Nov., 1987.

28   See, for example, C.L.R. James and Eric Williams, *Capitalism and Slavery,* London, Andre Deutsch, 1964.

29 This is one of the main arguments of Madan Sarup, *Marxism, Structuralism, Education*, Lewis, Falmer, 1983.

30 Historians have shown how, in a period of unprecedented change, the public image of the British monarchy was fundamentally transformed in the years before the First World War. The old ceremonial was successfully adapted in response to the changed domestic and international situation, and new rituals were self- consciously invented. Gradually the monarchy became a symbol of consensus and continuity. At a time of internal unrest and international revolution the monarchy became associated with uniqueness, tradition and permanence. The role of the monarchy has been to create a comforting picture of stability. See David Cannadine, 'The Context, Performance and Meaning of Ritual: The British Monarchy and the Invention of Tradition', in Eric Hobsbawm and Terence Ranger, (eds.), *The Invention of Tradition*, Cambridge, Cambridge University Press, 1983.

31 For the view that metaphors are a part of speech that affect the ways in which we perceive, think and act, see George Lakoff and Mark Johnson, *Metaphors We Live By* Chicago, The University of Chicago Press, 1980.

Chapter 9: Ideology and politics

1   John Merrington, 'Theory and Practice in Gramsci's Marxism', in *Western Marxism: A Critical Reader,* London, New Left Review, 1977, p.142.

2   Robert Bocock, *Hegemony,* London, Tavistock, 1986.

3   Carl Boggs, *Gramsci's Marxism,* London, Pluto, 1976, p.53.

4   James Donald and Stuart Hall, (eds.), *Politics and Ideology,* Milton Keynes, Open University, p.xii. The section on politics and nationalism is particularly useful.

5   Perry Anderson, 'The Antinomies of Antonio Gramsci', in *New Left Review* Number 100, November 1976-January 1977, p.6.

6.   Antonio Gramsci, *Selections from the Prison Notebooks,* London, Lawrence and Wishart, 1971. For an excellent survey of his political theory see Anne Sassoon, *Gramsci's Politics,* 2nd edition, London, Hutchinson 1981. It contains a useful postscript which discusses education, intellectuals, and specialized knowledge.

7   Stuart Hall, 'The rediscovery of 'ideology': return of the repressed in media studies' in Michael Gurevitch, et al., *Culture, Society and the Media,* London, Methuen, 1982, p.67. I am much indebted to Hall's work.

8   Ibid., p.77. V.N. Volosinov, *Marxism and the Philosophy of Language,* New York, Seminar Press, 1973.

9   Louis Althusser, 'Ideology and Ideological State Apparatuses', in *Lenin and Philosophy and other Essays,* London, New Left Books, p.160.

10   Gregor McLennan, et al., 'Althusser's Theory of Ideology', in Centre for Contemporary Cultural Studies, *On Ideology,* London, Hutchinson, 1978, p.96. A criticism that could be made of Althusser's theory of ideology is that it tended to present the process as too uni-accentual, too functionally adapted to the reproduction of the dominant ideology. The work of Volosinov and Gramsci offered a significant correction to this functionalism by reintroducing into the domain of ideology and language the notion of a 'struggle over meaning'.

11   Ernesto Laclau, *Politics and Ideology in Marxist Theory,* London, New Left Books, 1977, p.99.

12   Ibid., pp.81-142.

13   This example is taken from Bill Schwarz, 'Conservatism, Nationalism and Imperialism', in James Donald and Stuart Hall, (eds.)., *Politics and Ideology,* op.cit., p.182.

14   A. Cutler, B. Hindess, P. Hirst, and A. Hussein, *Marx's Capital and Capitalism Today,* London, Routledge & Kegan Paul, 1977, 2 vols. For a critique of Althusser's theory of ideology see Paul Hirst, *On Law and Ideology,* London, Macmillan, 1979.

15   Ernesto Laclau and Chantal Mouffe, *Hegemony and Socialist Strategy: Towards a Radical Democratic Politics*, London, Verso, 1985.

16   Normal Geras, 'Post-Marxism?', *New Left Review*, No.163, May/June 1987, p.49. For a reply to Geras see Ernesto Laclau/Chantal Mouffe, 'Post-Marxism without Apologies', *New Left Review*, No.166, November/December 1987. The debate was continued by Nicos Mouzelis, 'Marxism or Post-Marxism?', *New Left Review*, No. 167, January/February 1988, and by Norman Geras, 'Ex-Marxism Without Substance: Being a Real Reply to Laclau and Mouffe', *New Left Review*, No. 169, May/June 1988.

Ernesto Laclau has an unfolding philosophical project which is to overcome the theoretical impasses of the Left. In his first book of essays *Politics and Ideology in Marxism* (1977) he criticised essentialism in Marxism. And then, in *Hegemony and Socialist Strategy* (1985) written with Chantal Mouffe, he expanded the Gramscian theory of hegemony. The essays in *New Reflections on the Revolution of Our Time* (1990) deal with many topics including the nature of history, subjectivity, and identity.

Laclau now considers himself a post-marxist. In his view Hegel and Marx reduce history to a rationality; everything that happens is rational and has to happen from within itself. (An analogy might be the statement: 'God is Almighty; everything is an example of his will'). Post-marxism starts with a different view of history. Laclau emphasises, something that Gramsci realised: the importance of the political. Laclau stresses the role of contingency (something which may or may not happen) and insists that contingency is not the random or the accidental. To put it concisely, there is no absolute necessity in history. History is contingent.

Laclau believes that we are living in a subjective society. In a peasant society the space for the development of subjectivity was limited; in disorganised capitalism, however, the element of subjectivity comes to the fore. We know that capitalism can only exist by a continual subversion of previously existing social relations. Disorganised capitalism leads to dislocation. There is now more fragmentation in society but at the same time, there are more possibilities for human emancipation.

In the 19th century, when most workers spent many hours in a factory, they possibly had an identity which was unified. But now people spend a lot of their time doing many things in different places, there is a decline in unified identities. There is now an increase, a proliferation of identities. The trade unions, in the past, fostered a narrow type of politics. Now, even workers' struggles are not class struggles. There is now a plurality of democratic struggles.

In short, Laclau's work is a critique of the foundamentalism found in Marxism and is antagonistic to the Hegelian and Marxist notion of the logic of history. He argues that it is impossible fully to grasp society in its totality. Moreover, he believes that subjects are not fully constituted, they are unclosed, unfinished. See Ernesto Laclau, *New Reflections on the Revol-*

ution of our Time, London, Verso 1990. For arguments against Laclau's Post-marxism, see Norman Geras, *Discourses of Extremity; Radical Ethnics and Post-Marxist Extravagances*, Verso, 1990.

17   Many thinkers now concede that Marx did not provide a theory of politics, and that there is a tension, within marxism, between voluntarism and determinism (for example, the concept of 'relative autonomy'). While I would agree that all social practices are linguistically mediated, I have some reservations about Laclau's concept of discourse. He has little to say about human needs and the economic level of society. Though Laclau is right to be concerned about subjectivity and the construction of political identities, his work does not contain a theory of subjectivity. Nor does he say anything about the problem of reactionary social identities. Laclau espouses 'radical democracy' but I believe that he antagonizes many people by associating it with 'post-marxism'. In short, Laclau's 'alliance' politics ignores the fact that the world is constructed by the logic of capital. It is capital that constructs the different forms of marginality. For further criticisms of Laclau and Mouffe see Ellen Meiksins Wood, *The Retreat from Class: A New 'True' Socialism*, London, Verso, 1986.

18   Hall writes that Thatcherite populism 'combines the resonant themes of organic Toryism — nation, family, duty, authority, standards, traditionalism — with the aggressive themes of a revived neo-liberalism — self interest, competitive individualism, anti-statism.' Stuart Hall and Martin Jacques, (eds.), *The Politics of Thatcherism*, London, Lawrence and Wishart, 1983, p.29.

19   Eric Hobsbawm, Labour's Lost Millions, *Marxism Today*, October 1983. *The Forward March of Labour Halted?* (edited by Martin Jaques and Francis Mulhern), London, Verso, 1981.

20   Alberto Melucci, 'The new social movements: A Theoretical Approach', *Social Science Information*, 19, no.2, 1980.

21   Manuel Castells, *The City and the Grassroots*, Edward Arnold, London, 1983.

22   Laclau and Mouffe are also against the Lukácsian view of the proletariat as the 'universal class'. They write, 'The basic obstacle, as we have seen, has been classism: that is to say, the idea that the working class represents the privileged agent in which the fundamental impulse of social change resides.' Ernesto Laclau and Chantal Mouffe, *Hegemony and Socialist Strategy: Towards a Radical Democratic Politics*, London, Verso, 1985, p.177.

23   Andre Gorz, *Farewell to the Working Class*, London, Pluto Press, 1982.

24   Paul Gilroy, *There Ain't No Black in the Union Jack: The cultural politics of race and nation*, London, Hutchinson, p.233.

25   During the last few years there have been an increasing number of disorders and riots in Britain. I would argue that the meaning of these events is often constructed after the events. Generally speaking, the *radical* perspective

assumes that change can come about through unrest. The *liberal* perspective (exemplified in the Scarman report) emphasizes the 'racial' disadvantages of black people and looks at their grievances. In contrast the *conservative* perspective assumes that the social structures are fair and adequate. There is no justification for disorder; urban unrest is irrational. Disorder is due to the actions of individual criminals, or comes about through outside (political) influences. In terms of social policy there is often talk of 'inner city regeneration'. A conservative social policy that emphasized unemployment would bring into question what they say about the causes of disorder. The government's main response to riots is to increase police training and provide more equipment. And so police tactics have become military tactics. Coercive policing means that the causes of social unrest are not dealt with; questions of economic injustice are marginalized. At the same time there is a co-option policy consisting of multi-agency policing, consultative committees, and so forth. This issue raises many questions. For example, in a society where social inequality is increasing, what is the source of social adhesion?

26   Paul Gilroy, op.cit., p.245.

Chapter 10: Education and social change

1   The family-education couple have a significant role in the social distribution of cultural 'capital'. As I mentioned in chapter 1, language plays an important role in the process.

2   Samuel Bowles and Herbert Gintis, *Schooling in Capitalist America*, London, Routledge, 1976, p.21.

3   10.5 per cent of the working population of the United Kingdom (about 2.8 million people) are unemployed. See *Britain 1988, an official handbook,* H.M.S.O.

4   No photograph has ever convinced or refuted anyone but it can confirm. See Roland Barthes, *Image-Music-Text,* London, Fontana, 1977.

5   A good source of information about materials is the journal *Multicultural Teaching,* it is obtainable from Trentham Books Ltd., 30 Wenger Crescent, Trentham, Stoke-on-Trent, Staff., England, ST4 8LE.

6   Very little work, as yet, has been done on this subject. See Robert Cons and Philip Dodd (eds.), *Englishness: Politics and Culture,* 1880-1920, London, Croom Helm, 1986. Dennis Walder (ed.), Literature in the Modern World, Oxford, Oxford University Press, 1990. This excellent Open Universoty Reader contains sections on Englishness, ideology and empire.

7   This is, of course, one of the functions of ideology; it shapes perceptions and preferences in such a way that social agents 'accept their role in the existing order of things, either because they can see or imagine no alternative to it, or because they see it as natural and unchangeable, or because they value it as divinely ordained or beneficial.' Steven Lukes, quoted in Stuart Hall, 'The rediscovery of ideology: return of the repressed in media studies', in Gurvitch et al (eds.), *Culture, Society and the Media,* London, Methuen, 1982, p.65.

8   See, for example, Jean-Francois Lyotard, *The Post-modern Condition: a Report on Knowledge*, Manchester, Manchester University Press, 1984.

9   Stuart Schneiderman, *Jacques Lacan: The Death of an Intellectual Hero*, Harvard University Press, 1983, p.174.

10 Some statistics: at the time of writing fewer than 2 per cent of teachers came from ethnic minorities. Only 2-5 per cent of all students graduating from teacher training institutions in 1980 were Afro-Caribbean or Asians. See *New Equals,* Number 27, Autumn 1987. The latest figures show that less than seven *police officers* out of every 1,000 comes from an Afro-Caribbean or Asian background. But black people are not underrepresented in every occupation or situation. *Prisoners* of Afro-Caribbean origin represent 8% of the male and 12% of the female prison population while they comprise less than 2% of the whole population. See *New Equals,* No.23, Winter 1986, pp.1-5. It is published by the Commission for Racial Equality, Elliot House, 10/12 Allington Street, London SW1E 5EH. Tel. 01-828 7022.

11   Paulo Freire, *Education for Critical Consciousness*, London, Sheed and Ward, 1974, p.73.

12   I have been very impressed by, and learnt much from, a film directed by Chen Kaige called *King of the Children* (China, 1987). Set during the years of the Cultural Revolution, the film concerns an inexperienced but strong-minded young man who is assigned to teach in a remote mountain village. He rejects rote learning and propaganda and encourages the children to understand the Chinese language, to write from their own experiences, and to build upon their own resources.

13   I. Bates, J. Clarke, P. Cohen, D. Finn, R. Moore, and P. Willis, *Schooling for the Dole? The New Vocationalism*, London, Macmillan, 1984, p.160.

14   Ibid., Philip Cohen, Against the New Vocationalism, p.142.

15   R. Johnson, 'Really useful Knowledge:: Radical Education and Working-Class Culture 1790-1845', in *Education and the State. Vol.2, Politics, Patriarchy and Practice*, Lewis, The Falmer Press, 1981.

16   It could be argued that capitalism has been so extraordinarily successful that its values permeate every institution. It has moved into education. It shapes culture. But, at the same time, capitalist development in the West has become not only anti- productive but dangerous. There is now a convergence of many destructive trends. Consider: the wasteful accumulation of armaments, the destruction of the ozone layer, the pollution of the environment, the devastation of the rain forests. There must be a critique of a system which can produce enormous wealth in the West and poverty in the 'Third World'. Why is there poverty even in the midst of wealthy nations? See, for example, Colin Lacey and Roy Williams (eds.), *Education, Ecology and Development. The Case for an Education Network*, Kogan Page, 1987.

17   Hayden White, *Tropics of Discourse*, Baltimore, John Hopkins University Press, 1978, and *Metahistory*, Baltimore, John Hopkins University Press, 1973.

18   O. Negt and A. Kluge, *Offentlichkeit und Erfahrung*, Frankfurt/Main, 1972.

19   Edward Said, 'Opponents, Audiences, Constituencies and Community', in H. Foster (ed.), *Postmodern Culture,* London, Pluto Press, 1985, p.158.

20   A point made by Stuart Hall, 'The dream of education for all — is it over?' in a lecture delivered at University of London Goldsmiths' College, 12th March, 1985.

References

BAKER, K. (1987) *Speech to the Annual Conference of the Conservative Party* 7 October, Blackpool.

CASHMORE, E. and TROYNA, B. (1990) *Introduction to Race Relations: Second Edition*, Lewes, The Falmer Press.

GILL, D. (1989/90) 'Introctrination, curriculum and the law', *Critical Social Policy*, 27, pp.56-72.

HATCHER, R. (1989) 'Anti-racist education after the Act', *Multicultural Teaching*, Vol. 7, No. 3, pp.26-27.

JOHNSON, R. (1989) 'Thatcherism and Englsih Education: Breaking the mould or confirming the pattern?' *History of Education*, Vol. 18, No. 2, pp.91-121.

JOSEPH, K. (1986) *Without Prejudice: Education for an Ethnically Mixed Society* 20 May (unpublished).

MORTIMORE, P. *et al.* (1988) *School Matters: The Junior Years*, Wells, Open Books.

MURPHY, J. (1985) 'Does the difference schools make, make a differnce?' *British Journal of Sociology*, Vol. 36, No. 1, pp.106-115.

NAIRN, T. (1977) *The Break-Up of Britain: Crisis and Neo-Nationalism*, London, New Left Books.

RAYNOR, J. (1989) 'A National or Nationalist Curriculum?' in B. Moon, P. Murphy and J. Raynor (eds), *Policies for the Curriculum*, London, Hodder and Stoughton, pp.45-50.

RUTTER, M. *et al* (1979) *Fifteen Thousand Hours*, Shepton Mallet, Open Books.

SAMUEL, R. (1989) 'Introduction: exciting to be English' in R. Samuel (ed), *Patriotism: The Making and Unmaking of British National Identity: Vol. 1 History and Politics*, London, Routledge, pp.xviii-lxvii.

SMITH, D. J. and TOMLINSON, S. (1989) *The School Effect: A Study of Multi-Racial Comprehensives*, London, Policy Studies Institute.

TEBBIT, N. (1990) 'Fanfare on being British', *The Field*, May, pp.76-78.

TROYNA, B. (1990) 'Reform or deform? The 1988 Education Reform Act and Racial Equality in Britain', *New Community*, Vol. 16, No. 3, pp.403-416.

TROYNA, B. abd CARRINGTON, B. (1990) *Education, Racism and Reform*, London, Routledge.

Index